Anarchism

A Marxist Criticism

John Molyneux

Bookmarks Publications

Anarchism: A Marxist Criticism
John Molyneux

First published in 2011 by Bookmarks Publications
c/o 1 Bloomsbury Street, London WC1B 3QE
© Bookmarks Publications

Typeset by Phil Whaite
Printed by Russell Press

ISBN 9781905192885

Contents

Introduction.. 1

1. The appeal of anarchism 7

2. Anarchist ideas... 10
   The state 11
   Leadership 19
   The party 23
   Individual, society and class 29

3. The record of anarchism 37
   Bakunin 37
   Russia 41
   Note on the anarchist critique of Bolshevism 47
   Spain... 50

4. Anarchism today... 55
   Lifestyle anarchism 55
   Autonomism 58
   Platform anarchism... 64
   Direct action 67
   Participation in elections... 70
   Decision making in the movement 72

5. The way forward 77

Suggestions for further reading 82

About the author

John Molyneux is a socialist writer and activist, formerly a lecturer a Portsmouth University and now living in Dublin. His publications include *Marxism and the Party* (1978), *What is the Real Marxist Tradition?* (1985) and *Rembrandt and Revolution* (2001). He is a member of the Socialist Workers Party in Britain and Ireland.

Acknowledgements

Thanks are due to Sally Campbell, Kieran Allen, Paul Blackledge, Mark Bergfeld, Alex Callinicos and Andy Durgan for critical comments and suggestions.

This work is dedicated, with love and gratitude, to my partner, Mary Smith.

Introduction

I was working on this booklet when the Tunisian and Egyptian Revolutions broke out in the winter of 2010-11, followed by epic struggles, still ongoing as I write, in Libya, Bahrain, Yemen and Syria. As I have had a long-standing involvement with the Egyptian left, these momentous events necessarily diverted my attention from the critique of anarchism for a while, but they were rapidly followed by developments which made this critique even more relevant and urgent, namely the occupations of the squares in Spain.

On 15 May 2011, taking inspiration from Tahrir Square in Cairo, thousands of Spaniards occupied Puerta Da Sol, the main square in Madrid, one week in advance of nationwide local elections. They were protesting at unemployment, homelessness and the whole corrupt political system. They called themselves *los indignados*—the indignant—and denounced all the mainstream politicians and parties. "They do not represent us!" was a key slogan and they demanded "Real democracy now!" Within days these occupations or camps had spread to over 100 cities right across the country including, crucially, Placa Catalunya in Barcelona. Spanish communities as far afield as Brussels and Dublin followed suit with solidarity rallies. On 19 June close to a million people, including 250,000 in Barcelona, marched in solidarity with *los indignados*. Moreover, on 25 May a similar camp was established in Syntagma Square in Athens which served as a focus for the ongoing mass protests and general strikes against the harsh austerity measures being imposed on the Greek people by the EU/IMF.

Taken as a whole this movement was young, peaceful, hugely vibrant and enthusiastic, and clearly influenced by various forms of anarchism or autonomism, or at least by anarchist or autonomist ideas. It took decisions by means of direct democracy in its general assemblies and all political parties, together with their banners, flags, newspapers, etc, were banned from the squares.

The struggle of *los indignados* is part of an international rising tide of struggle in response to the global crisis of capitalism that broke out with the collapse of Lehman Brothers in August 2008, which has already included the sustained resistance of the Greek working class, the French workers' fight over pensions, the British student revolt in late 2010, the truly amazing revolutions in Tunisia and Egypt and the rest of the Arab Spring, the mass movement in Wisconsin, and the British workers' huge demonstration of 26 March and strikes of 30 June, and much else besides. Hopefully, by the time this booklet is published, more struggles will have developed.

In such a situation an upsurge of anarchist or anarchist-inspired ideas and moods is almost inevitable. It was the same in the great struggles of 1968, particularly in the May Events in Paris and in the general student movement of that time, and again in the international anti-capitalist movement that began in Seattle in 1999. The characteristic themes of anarchism—its blanket rejection of the state and authority, of corrupt parliamentary politics and self-serving political parties—resonate powerfully with the spontaneous rebellion of the young and the newly radicalised. This is especially the case when there is such a big vacuum on the left created by the historic decline and disappearance of the old Communist Parties and the profound shift to the right by the traditional social democratic parties (still epitomised by the odious figure of Tony Blair, best friend of Bush and Berlusconi). Moreover, it is many ways a very welcome development, bringing imagination and flair to the movement including new tactics and an expanded sense of the possible, much preferable to the dead hand of bureaucracy and routine.

But this is not to say that these anarchist ideas constitute an adequate guide to action for the movement—unfortunately they do not. (I say unfortunately because if they did it would save no end of political labour, much of it tedious.) As a socialist and Marxist I would say that every "leftist", every socialist, every would-be revolutionary should work in and with these anarchist-influenced movements in a spirit of solidarity, cooperation and readiness to learn—the great Marxists, beginning with Marx, have always *learned* from the movement—but they also need to discuss and try to persuade because anarchist ideas, including autonomist ideas (autonomism is really closer to anarchism than it is to Marxism), have certain *fundamental* weaknesses. Obviously this booklet is concerned with demonstrating those weaknesses, but here I just want to give some examples of them drawn from the most recent experience.

First, the struggle in Spain. As noted above, the main slogans of this movement were "They [the government and the politicians] do not represent us" and "Real democracy now!" Popularising these slogans was a great achievement. They cut to the heart of the sham that is parliamentary democracy, where every four or five years the people get to choose which set of politicians will lie to them, misrepresent them and rob them, while real power remains unelected and unaccountable in the boardrooms of the corporations and offices of the state bureaucracy. However, there was also a serious problem. *Los indignados* could demand "real democracy", but how were they actually going to get it? Clearly it was not a demand that could be won just by asking for it; the establishment of "real" democracy, by which the protesters meant "direct democracy", would require at the very least the Spanish government and state apparatus to voluntarily dissolve themselves. Of course the movement could reply that it was creating its own real democracy through the general assemblies in the squares, and again this was an impressive achievement, but it only provided democratic control of the squares, not of the wider society. It offered no power whatsoever over the economy, the police, the army or any of the main levers of power in Spanish society, and no strategy or route to such power.

Actually establishing real democracy in the society, and not just temporarily in the squares, would involve, at a minimum: (a) displacing or dismantling the existing state system and replacing it with one based on direct democracy; and (b) amassing and mobilising the popular power capable of bringing about this change, ie a revolution, despite the inevitable resistance of the rich and all the established authorities. This, in turn, would require developing a political strategy for reaching and drawing into action the majority of ordinary working people not only on the streets but also in their workplaces where economic power is based. In other words it would involve going beyond the simple rejection of the state, of leadership and of political organisation that are the typical characteristics of anarchism.

Second, the revolution in Egypt. At first glance this revolution might seem to confirm anarchism's wildest dreams: a hated tyrant brought down by a mass spontaneous revolt of the people, involving intense street fighting, predominantly the young, mobilised via Facebook and Twitter. And indeed there is a degree of truth in this picture. Most great revolutions (including the French Revolution, the Paris Commune and the Russian Revolution) *begin* spontaneously and the Egyptian Revolution so far has not been directed or led by any single party or political force. But it is also true that closer inspection reveals a lot of hard political organisation behind and within the overall spontaneity.

The revolt that started on 25 January 2011 did not come out of the blue. It was sparked by the success of the Tunisian Revolution on 14 January but it was prepared over a number of years by a combination of democratic, anti-imperialist and workers' struggles. In these struggles anarchist ideas had little influence, but political parties, including the Muslim Brotherhood, the Nasserite Karama Party and the Revolutionary Socialists, played a substantial role. Moreover, the strike wave of 2008 saw the emergence of independent trade unions (the previous unions were controlled by the Mubarak regime) which have developed further in the course of the revolution. In the revolution itself these parties continued to be actively engaged and others have been created.

Particularly interesting is the part played by the Muslim Brotherhood, which was by far the largest opposition party in Egypt. Under the dictatorship the Muslim Brotherhood was a cautious moderate reformist party, Islamic but not extreme fundamentalist or terrorist. In some ways it more closely resembled the British Labour Party than it did Al Qaida, but it was illegal and frequently subject to persecution. It opposed the initial demonstration on 25 January but as the revolution gathered mass support it yielded to pressure and allowed its younger members to participate. All accounts suggest that the Muslim Brotherhood youth then played a heroic role in fighting the police and in defending Tahrir Square against the pro-Mubarak thugs in the life and death struggle that was the Battle of the Camel on 2 February. When Mubarak fell and was replaced by the military junta the Brotherhood switched to supporting the government and opposing further protests, but this has led to many of its youth splitting away. Moreover, as I write these lines (on Friday 8 July) there is a mass occupation of Tahrir Square, involving something like 20 political parties, calling for the pace of the revolution to be speeded up, and the Brotherhood have said they support it!

Anyone who wants to see the Egyptian Revolution continue, who wants to see it move towards "real democracy" and, indeed, the overthrow of capitalism, has to deal, strategically and tactically, with these contradictions, just as they also have to know how to work with the developing independent trade unions and how to combine democratic demands with social and economic demands so as to focus and unite the huge revolutionary energy of the newly awakened Egyptian masses. Unfortunately, dealing with contradictions and operating strategically and tactically are not anarchism's strong points, and a blanket rejection of all political parties, trade unions and flags a la the Spanish *indignados* would succeed only in completely isolating those who proposed it. Nor in Egypt today is it an option to sit with folded arms and say we have to wait until the mass of Egyptian workers free themselves from their various illusions in religion, the army and bourgeois democracy and become true anarchists. Long before that can happen the revolutionary moment will have been let slip and it is likely that the socialists, the revolutionaries—be they anarchist, Trotskyist, Leninist or whatever—will all find themselves in Egyptian jails.

In other words, current events confirm the basic argument of this booklet, that the experience of the last 150 years shows beyond all reasonable doubt that, despite their very considerable merits, anarchist ideas (in all their various forms) do not constitute a viable way to change the world.

1. The appeal of anarchism

Anarchism has always had a strong appeal for those people who rebel against this rotten society. In particular it appeals to the young, which is very much to its credit. In every radical and revolutionary movement the young have played a disproportionate role, for it is the young, unbroken and unbowed, who possess the highest levels of energy, enthusiasm and idealism.

In the face of rampant exploitation and injustice, the overwhelming power of the capitalist state and the stifling grip of its ideology anarchism hurls a defiant "No". It says we do not have to live like this. There does not have to be rich and poor, exploiters and exploited, rulers and ruled. There does not have to be war, racism, oppression and there doesn't have to be domination of the majority by the minority or even of the minority by the majority.

Against the ceaseless indoctrination which holds that the mass of people are by nature either stupid or self-seeking and therefore have to be told what to do and kept in line by a higher authority, anarchism asserts that we have the potential to live cooperatively and harmoniously.

Anarchism rejects with contempt the hypocrisy and cynical opportunism of bourgeois (establishment) politics where politicians package and sell themselves like soap powder, and where policies are placed at the mercy of the opinion polls without a shred of principle. In particular anarchism represents a reaction to the progressive incorporation of the main left and opposition parties within this corrupt world of official politics. It gives radical expression to the widespread perception among ordinary people that all politicians are the same: just wanting power for themselves and to line their own pockets.

In present circumstances therefore it is not surprising that anarchism has enjoyed something of a resurgence right across Europe. Seldom if ever in its history has reformist socialism or social democracy so openly abandoned any idea of challenging the system, or stood so clearly revealed as merely an accomplice of the state. Even more important has been the disintegration of the so-called Communist regimes in Eastern Europe and Russia. Throughout the world millions of people saw these countries as embodying the actually existing alternative to Western capitalism, but the events of 1989-92 mercilessly exposed this illusion, demonstrating not only the abysmal failure of the bureaucratic command economies but also the immense popular hatred of the regimes. Stalinism, the tradition which for 60 years dominated so much of the left internationally, more or less collapsed and the resulting demoralisation spread far beyond the ranks of the Communist Parties themselves to all those who saw the East as in some way superior to Western capitalism. In this situation it was to be expected that anarchism would be seen by some of those looking for a radical alternative as the only ideology still with clean hands.

Anarchism also has a substantial appeal as the ideological rationale of a certain lifestyle. To a layer of young people living largely in poverty, frequently unemployed, often homeless or squatting or in the poorest rented accommodation, existing more or less in the margins of society in the run down areas of the inner cities, anarchism symbolises their rejection of a system that has rejected them.

Possession of noble aims and a powerful and varied appeal does not, however, guarantee that an ideology actually has the potential to achieve the aims it proclaims. Stalinism, for instance, had immense appeal to opponents of capitalism and imperialism, but proved to be a complete dead end. So is anarchism an ideology capable of guiding the struggle for human emancipation to a victorious conclusion?

This booklet will argue that it is not, that the basic ideas of anarchism are seriously flawed and result in a practice that can hamper the liberation struggle. It will present a critique of anarchist theory and practice from a Marxist standpoint (ie the standpoint of the classical Marxism of Marx, Lenin and Trotsky, not Stalinism) and argue that only Marxism points the road to the classless free society of the future that both Marxists and anarchists share as their ultimate goal.

2. Anarchist ideas

Anarchism comes in many forms. There is pure individualist anarchism which rejects all forms of organisation. There are numerous small anarchist organisations. There are anarchists who proclaim their faith in the people regardless of class. There are communist anarchists who look to the working class. There is the anarchism of the peasant band in the tradition of Makhno (the peasant leader in Russia during the civil war that followed the revolution). There is anarchism which dismisses the trade unions. There is anarcho-syndicalism which bases itself on workers' unions. There are revolutionary anarchists, terrorist anarchists, pacifist anarchists, green anarchists. There are anarchists who fit none of these categories or have their own unique permutation of all of them.

There are anarchists influenced by Proudhon, by Bakunin, by Kropotkin, but there are no Proudhonists, Bakuninists or Kropotkinists who follow a specific doctrine or line. To the critic therefore anarchism presents a moving target. Attack a particular theory or policy and most anarchists will turn out not to share it. Dissect the ideas of a particular classic thinker and other anarchists will disown him.

Nevertheless, there are certain general ideas and attitudes which are common to all or most versions of anarchism and which can serve as the point of departure for a critique. The most important of these are: (a) hostility to the state in all its forms, including the idea of a revolutionary state; (b) hostility to leadership in all its forms, including revolutionary leadership; (c) hostility to all political parties, including the idea of a revolutionary party; and (d) a tendency to individualism. I shall consider each of these in turn.

The state

The literal meaning of anarchy is "no rule", and opposition to the state and government—not just to a particular state or particular government but to all states and all governments at all times, as a matter of principle—is the defining characteristic of anarchism as a creed.

Anarchism maintains that the very existence of a state, ie of special bodies of men (and women) exercising legal and physical power over society as a whole, is oppressive and incompatible with real human freedom. To end oppression and establish freedom the rule of the state must be replaced by that of the self-governing community without any over-riding central authority.

According to conventional wisdom such a perspective is either disastrous or impossible. Disastrous because without the state society would descend into a chaotic "war of all against all" in which the so-called "law of the jungle" would prevail and human life would be "nasty, brutish and short" (as the 17th century political philosopher Thomas Hobbes once put it). Impossible because it is "human nature" that some individual or group of individuals would inevitably rise to the top and establish themselves as rulers. The best that can be hoped for therefore is to make the state democratic by electing the government and maintaining certain democratic rights (freedom of speech, etc).

However, conventional wisdom is wrong about this and anarchism is right. Anthropology provides clear proof that human beings can live in societies without state or government and that such societies, far from being chaotic, are as or more ordered than our own. Many such ancephalous (headless) societies have been witnessed and studied by anthropologists—excellent examples are the !Kung San or Kalahari Bushmen of Southern Africa—and there are good reasons for believing that statelessness was the norm for the hundreds and thousands of years between the origins of human society and its division into classes with the advent of agriculture, herding and private property between 10,000 and 5,000 years ago.

Anarchism is also right in seeing all forms of the state as involving the oppression of one group in society by another. The advent of parliamentary democracy does not change this. Parliaments, no matter how they are elected, do not hold real power, which remains concentrated in the hands of the permanent officials of the state (generals, police chiefs, judges, civil servants, etc), bankers and big business who use that power to serve their own interests, not the interests of ordinary people.

But if a stateless society is both possible and desirable how is the existing state to be got rid of? It is in dealing with this crucial question that anarchism begins to run into trouble.

Some anarchists, it must be said, do not even attempt to answer it. They are content with rejection of the authority of the state as a purely personal attitude and feel no need to formulate a coherent strategy for its abolition. But such a stance is both a cop-out in that it leaves the state free to carry on with its oppression of the mass of people in perpetuity and self-defeating in that no individual or small group can ultimately resist the power of the state.

Some anarchists attempt to escape the authority of the state via small self-governing communities in the countryside or even in the inner cities. Unfortunately the anarchist commune suffers from the same difficulties as the socialist commune advocated by Robert Owen and the utopian socialists more than 150 years ago: (a) it is only a practical proposition for a small minority; and (b) the minority concerned remain subject to all the pressures of wider society and sooner or later (usually sooner rather than later) succumb to them.

However, the most radical and the most serious answer to this question is that the state will be destroyed by revolution, ie by a mass popular uprising in which the working class through its own direct action will smash up and disintegrate the core institutions of the existing state—the armed forces, the police, the courts, the prisons, etc.

From a Marxist standpoint this is absolutely correct— Lenin devoted his most important theoretical work *The State and Revolution* to arguing precisely that the essence of revolution was this smashing of the state machine (as opposed to the social democratic and reformist notion of taking over the existing state). Moreover, it has the advantage of being a process that has actually occurred historically, first in the Paris Commune of 1871, then in the Russian Revolution of 1917, while every great popular revolution, whether it be the German Revolution of 1918-23, the Spanish Revolution of 1936 or the Iranian Revolution of 1979, shows tendencies in this direction.

But the smashing of the old state machine immediately raises the question of what is to replace it. Anarchism has tended to be very vague on this point, but the only answer consistent with anarchist principles is that the old state must be replaced straight away by a self-governing stateless community with no government or central authority. Here the anarchist position loses all credibility. It is one thing to assert, as Marxism does, that once socialism has definitely established itself internationally and classes and class struggle have disappeared and production has reached a level where the necessities of life are provided for all and where the habit of work for the collective good has become second nature, then the state will lose its functions and wither away. It is quite another thing to propose that in the midst of revolution, when the success of the revolution hangs by a thread, the revolutionary class should dispense immediately with all use of power.

There are two fundamental reasons why this would be disastrous. The first is that it takes no account of the inevitable resistance of the old ruling class. The class struggle does not cease with the success of the uprising. The history of *every* revolution shows that not only will the old ruling class stop at nothing to retain the power it has got, but it will also stop at nothing to try to regain the power it has lost. Given the unlikelihood of simultaneous international revolution it must also be born in mind that the dispossessed bourgeoisie will be able to count on support from governments and reactionary forces abroad.

A successful revolution must reckon on facing everything from bureaucratic non-cooperation and economic sabotage to armed resistance, terrorism, civil war and foreign military intervention. Can a revolutionary people defend the revolution against such counter-revolutionary activity without the aid of a workers' militia or army, without any form of legal system to ensure that the will of the people is respected, without a system of centralised decision making and authority, that is without creating a revolutionary form of state power? No, it cannot.

There are many historical precedents to prove this, but let us take a hypothetical example. Let us assume a revolution in France which was met by a right wing uprising based in Marseilles, combined with incursions in the north east by right wing bands supported by the German and American governments. To defend itself the revolution would have to decide what forces to concentrate in the north east and what to send to Marseilles as well as how to supply them and arm them. This would have to be a national decision made by a national government. Failure to coordinate such decisions would simply be a recipe for defeat.

The second reason a revolutionary state is essential is to establish the new economic order. An enormous amount would be done by initiative from below in the shape of factory occupations, workers' control of industry, setting up of distribution cooperatives and so on, but a state would still be indispensable at this early stage.

Consider, for example, the problem of who would own the industries and factories expropriated from the capitalists. If these businesses were owned not by the new state but by the workers of each separate enterprise, this would not only hamper cooperation and planning but also lead to competition between different workplaces which would divide the working class, just when it had the greatest need for unity.

Or take the example of the railways. This was used by Frederick Engels, arguing against anarchism, over 138 years ago. He wrote:

> Here too the cooperation of an infinite number of individuals is absolutely necessary, and this cooperation must be practised during precisely fixed hours so that no accidents may happen. Here, too, the first condition of the job is a dominant will that settles all subordinate questions, whether this will is represented by a single delegate or a committee charged with the execution of the resolutions of the majority of persona interested (F Engels, "On Authority", 1872, http://www.marxists.org/archive/marx/works/1872/10/authority.htm).

These arguments clearly still apply. You could have massive input from the workers in each locality, in London, Manchester and Newcastle or Hamburg, Berlin and Munich, but when it came to timetabling or building new lines, there would have to be some overall coordination and authority. Think of planes and the need becomes even clearer and more urgent.

Nor will it do to say the industries would simply be the property of the whole community. This would be fine at a later stage, when a genuinely united community would exist, but in the midst of revolution the "community" is divided into opposed and warring classes and factions—it is therefore absolutely necessary for the revolutionary community, the working class, to have institutions which embody its interests.

Or take the question of the unemployed, the sick and others who presently live on state benefits. In a fully developed socialist (or anarchist) society unemployment will disappear and goods will be distributed according to need but in the immediate aftermath of revolution millions of people dependent on state benefits will inevitably continue to exist and will starve unless they are paid. Benefits are paid out of taxes levied on the wage earning population; therefore there will have to be an authority with the power to collect taxes in the weeks and months following the revolution. Therefore there will have to be a state.

The weakness of anarchism here is that all too often it has a romantic conception of revolution in which after "the great day" all difficulties are solved merely by goodwill. In a revolution many millions of working people act together to change society and in the process change themselves—their political and social awareness, their sense of themselves as part of a collective, is transformed and enormously expanded. Without this the new society cannot be built. But the process of transformation is not and cannot be either total or even, for the simple reason that not all sections of the working class will be involved in the struggle to the same degree and some it may bypass altogether. This will be even truer of the millions who make up the lower middle classes. Thus for a period after the revolution there will be a portion of the population who in their general outlook or on particular issues are still influenced by the old ideas or follow the lead of the old ruling class. Such people will sometimes have to be obliged, if necessary by law, to accept the majority decisions, and that implies a workers' state.

In principle it is the same as when workers on strike organise a picket line to prevent a minority of their own ranks from scabbing. In the final analysis a workers' state is simply a picket line raised to the highest possible level.

Some anarchists will argue, however, that the moment you have a state, it will mean a privileged elite corrupted by power which will soon evolve into a new tyranny. But this ignores the fact that the working class has repeatedly demonstrated its ability to create organs of revolutionary power which are completely different in form and content from the old capitalist state and are both democratic and egalitarian.

The Paris Commune of 1871 established the principles that all public officials should be elected, should be subject to recall and should be paid workers' wages. This greatly inhibits the participation of careerists and helps to prevent elected representatives developing interests separate from those they represent. The soviet or workers' council, which first appeared in St Petersburg in the 1905 Revolution ("soviet" was just the Russian word for council), and then spread across Russia in 1917, took this a stage further by having delegates elected from workplaces. This further enhanced the element of control from below by making representatives responsible to collectives where democratic discussion and debate could take place.

The electors in a parliamentary constituency, which is a largish geographical area, cannot control or remove their member of parliament, even if that politician breaks all their election promises or completely changes their political allegiance, because the electors are an atomised collection of individuals who never meet and so cannot form a collective will or make a collective decision. An excellent example of this was provided by the 2010 general election in Britain. Millions of people voted for the Liberal Democrats in order, so they thought, to keep out the Tories, only to see the Lib Dems form a coalition with

David Cameron's Tories and launch a massive assault on the welfare state. But there is nothing the electors can do about this, short of extra-parliamentary action, for about four years, by which time the damage will have been done. With workers' councils based on elections in workplaces all that would be needed would be to convene a workplace meeting and recall the representative.

Sometimes the objection is made that such a system would be undemocratic because it would exclude those not in workplaces—the unemployed, pensioners, homeworkers, etc. But this is not so. Provided the workers' councils are *based* on workplaces, where workers' collective power is concentrated, there is no reason why they should not include representatives from, say, the unemployed workers' associations, the pensioners' associations, tenants' or residents' groups and so on. In fact every section of the people, except exploiters and fascists, could and should be represented. Moreover, workers' councils would probably contain a number of different parties or groupings representing different trends or shades of opinion among the working people. They are not at all a recipe for a one party state or dictatorship. On the contrary they would be far more democratic and facilitate far more participation by ordinary working class people than any parliamentary system.

Since the Russian Revolution workers' councils have appeared in the German Revolution in 1918-19, in Italy in 1920, in Hungary in 1956, and in embryonic form in Chile in 1972, in Iran in 1979 and in Poland in 1980. The Popular Committees for the Defence of the Revolution, which emerged in the Egyptian Revolution of 2011, could also develop in this direction.

Workers' councils are not created according to a pre-established blueprint, but arise spontaneously from the struggle. They are the logical form of organisation adopted by the working class when its struggle begins to challenge the system as a whole. They represent the core of the new workers' state that will replace the old capitalist state and begin the transition to a classless society in which the state will wither away.

The fundamental point is this. The state is most definitely not an eternal institution but neither is it just a mistake or a bad idea which somehow lodged itself in the mind of humanity holding us all in thrall until anarchism arrived on the scene to explain it was not needed. The state arises from certain economic and social conditions—first and foremost the division of society into antagonistic classes on the basis of a low level of the productive forces—and it cannot be abolished until these real conditions have been changed. Moreover, to change these conditions a new revolutionary form of the state is necessary.

Leadership

Anarchists frequently proclaim their rejection of the idea of leadership. This is understandable. In capitalist society the ruling class has always thought of itself as born to lead and "leadership" is one of the prime qualities it tries to foster in its offspring through the various elite educational establishments. In this context leadership is associated with arrogance, bullying and privilege. Anarchists are right to react against it.

Nor does the leadership of the left in the labour and trade union movement present an attractive picture. Throughout the 20th century and into this one, becoming a "socialist" or social democratic leader has been synonymous with moderation and social climbing. The normal pattern is for an activist to start by building up support at the grass roots with radical sounding policies and rhetoric and rise gradually to prominence, shedding principles as they go, until he or she emerges as a fully-fledged member of the political elite, complete with smart suits, chauffeur driven car, high salary, business connections and innumerable other perks, a complete prisoner of the establishment they set out to change.

It is more or less the same with the trade union leader. From the moment he (it usually is *he*) becomes an official he leaves behind the grim conditions of the shop floor for the comfort of the office. His pay and hours cease to be linked to those of the workers he represents and he starts to accumulate privileges. His job is to mediate between workers and management and in the process he spends more time in the company of the latter than the former. Corruption, in the political if not the financial sense, is more or less inevitable. Before long he comes to see disputes and strikes as problems to be solved, not battles to be won, and the best way of solving them is to negotiate the minimum deal that the workforce can be cajoled or bullied into accepting.

Leadership of this kind is politically disastrous. At moments of great upheaval when large masses of working people start to become involved, start to take things into their own hands, the immediate instinct of such leaders is to try to calm things down and restore normality. If that means betraying the cause they are supposed to represent then so be it.

The events of May 1968 in France are a classic example. This extraordinary spontaneous mass movement of students and workers challenged the Gaullist regime through mass battles on the streets of Paris, student occupations and a nationwide general strike of ten million workers combined with numerous factory occupations. The "leaders", which meant at that time predominantly the leaders of the Communist Party and the CGT, could think of nothing better to do than to narrow down this potentially revolutionary movement to a series of modest demands on pay and conditions and get everybody back to work as soon as possible.

From experiences like this, which have been repeated time and time again in the history of the working class struggle and the revolutionary movement, it is easy to draw the conclusion that leadership as such is at fault and should be done away with. Unfortunately there is an insuperable problem with this position, namely that leadership is a fact. Moreover it is a fact which derives not from a wrong idea in people's heads or from the innate wickedness of certain individuals or from particular organisational structures but from the fact that people differ in their experiences, and therefore in their levels of political consciousness, commitment, knowledge, courage and so on.

In every workplace, every trade union branch, every campaign, there are some people more willing and able than others to take on responsibility for necessary tasks, for making the keynote speech, minding the contact list, looking after the money or, crucially, providing some idea of the political way forward.

Even the most spontaneous riots, demonstrations, strikes and uprisings, where history records no formal leadership or organisation, will, if placed under a microscope, reveal informal moments and structures of leadership: the person who shouts "forward" at the crucial moment; those who push their way to the front of the crowd; the individual who first throws a stone, etc.

This also affects anarchism. No matter how much anarchists may forswear leadership, the fact is that anarchist movements have always had leaders and that the history of anarchism, like the history of socialism or conservatism for that matter, is in part a history of its leading figures—Proudhon, Bakunin, Kropotkin, Makhno, Goldman, Voline, Durutti, even Daniel Cohn-Bendit. The fact that anarchist movements may formally refuse to acknowledge the existence of leaders doesn't ease the problem; it increases it. It means that anarchist leaders, not being formally elected, cannot be deselected or subjected to democratic control. It means that anarchist movements are peculiarly vulnerable to the self-appointed, self-perpetuating leader or even the leader appointed by the media (the spontaneist student movements of the 1960s suffered considerably from such media promoted "stars"). Indeed it is striking how often anarchist movements have been known, historically, simply by the name of their leaders. Who today, other than the scholar, could actually provide the formal name of Bakunin's movement, or Makhno's or Durutti's? By comparison the Communist Party, the First International, the Bolshevik Party and even the Socialist Workers Party are relatively well known.

If anarchism is incapable of resolving the problem of its own leadership, still less is it able to resolve the problem of the leadership of the working class as a whole. Historically this leadership has rested either with social democracy or Stalinism—a fact which has led to innumerable betrayals and defeats from the Second International's collapse into nationalism and support for imperialist war in 1914, to capitulation to Hitler in 1933, down to Tony Blair and New Labour's enthusiastic embrace of neoliberalism, George Bush and the Iraq war. Anarchism by its very existence constitutes a challenge to the hegemony of these forces. By the very act of producing books, pamphlets, papers, leaflets or even making speeches anarchism does battle for influence over the left and the working class. However, in so far as it rejects leadership as such and therefore fails to fight politically and organisationally for leadership of the class, it contributes not to the liberation of the working class from leaders but to the continued dominance of the reformist misleaders.

Nor will it do to try to sweep the whole issue under the carpet with phrases such as "Leadership doesn't matter; it's what the masses do that counts". The bourgeois view of history, in line with its general elitism and individualism, undoubtedly exaggerates the role of leadership out of all proportion, till history becomes reduced to a procession of kings, emperors, generals and presidents, and a Marxist, least of all, can afford to forget this. But the actions of leaders make a difference. Leaders cannot conjure revolutions out of thin air or create mass movements through will power; indeed they cannot make revolutions at all; only the masses can do that. But given the existence of a mass movement and a revolutionary situation the role played by the leadership of that movement can significantly affect the outcome and even on occasion make the difference between victory and defeat.

In Germany in the years of Hitler's rise to power (1929-33) there existed a mass workers' movement whose allegiance was divided between the SPD (Social Democrats) and the KPD (Communists). Had this movement united its forces it would have had the power to stop the Nazis. The fact that the Social Democrat leaders wanted, as usual, to avoid a confrontation and that the Communist leaders were under orders from Stalin to concentrate their fire on the Social Democrats not the Nazis, prevented such unity being forged and greatly assisted Hitler's march to power.

Thus, since the problem of leadership can neither be ignored nor wished away, there remains only one alternative for those who seriously want to change society, that is to work to build a genuinely revolutionary leadership which is: (a) under the democratic control of its supporters; (b) resistant to corruption by the system; and (c) able to identify the correct way forward in the struggle. Anarchism's theoretical confusion on the issue and its anti-leadership fetish mean it is incapable of performing this task.

The party

The question of revolutionary leadership leads directly to the question of the revolutionary party. However, anarchist opposition to the idea of the party is if anything even more intense than its hostility to the state and to leadership.

Once again this is very understandable. The fact that

parties, claiming to be Marxist, Leninist and workers' parties, have been the principal instruments of oppression and exploitation of hundreds of millions of working people in the so-called Communist states is bound to produce a general "anti-party" reaction. When one adds to this the conservative, bureaucratic and careerist nature of the social democratic and reformist parties and the rather ludicrous sectarianism of some far left would-be parties, widespread suspicion of the whole idea of a party is perhaps inevitable.

Nevertheless the fact remains that the building of a revolutionary party of the working class is essential both for the waging of day to day class struggle and even more so for the success of the future revolution.

There are two simple and compelling reasons for this. The first is that the working class confronts an enemy which is highly organised and centralised and therefore to defeat it must organise its own ranks. This is true in every workplace and industry where workers face the centralised power of capital and where the organisation and unity in action of the workforce is the first condition of any successful resistance. Workers who attempt to challenge their bosses as individuals without the power of collective organisation will simply be sacked. It is even truer at the level of society as a whole where the rule of the bosses is protected by that most highly centralised organisation, the capitalist state. This need for organisation is understood by every worker with the least amount of class and political consciousness and therefore those anarchists who reject organisation altogether condemn themselves to complete isolation from the working class.

The second compelling reason for a revolutionary party is that working class political consciousness always develops unevenly. Capitalist control of the media, the education system, the churches and innumerable other institutions ensures that in "normal" times, ie outside of periods of mass revolutionary struggle, capitalist ideology exerts a powerful influence on the thinking of the majority of workers.

It would be quite wrong to depict the mass of workers as completely brainwashed into passively accepting all that capitalism throws at them—their experience of exploitation, oppression, poverty, unemployment, etc, ensures that this is not the case. Nevertheless it remains true that bourgeois ideas have a powerful grip inside the working class. Typically working class consciousness is a contradictory combination of critical ideas that derive from their own experience and reactionary ideas imposed on them from above. For example, many workers will hate their boss and understand that there is one law for the rich and another for the poor, and yet also adopt racist, sexist and other prejudices. Other workers may be anti-racist and anti-sexist, and yet still believe that industry could not run without the profit motive. In normal times only a minority of workers consistently reject capitalist ideas.

That is why it is essential that there is a political organisation basing itself on this minority of politically conscious workers to wage the battle for revolutionary ideas inside the overall movement of the working class and the oppressed.

It is for this reason that the strategy adopted by many anarchists who do accept the need for working class organisation—the strategy of anarcho-syndicalism—remains inadequate. Anarcho-syndicalism counterposes to the idea of a Marxist political party the idea of revolutionary trade unionism. This is a step forward from individualist anarchism in that it does at least attempt to engage with the working class, but it is not enough.

Trade unions are essentially mass organisations formed by workers to bargain and fight over wages and conditions within the framework of capitalist relations of production. To perform this function effectively they have to have a membership which is as broad and all inclusive as possible.

Ideally a trade union will include in its ranks every worker in the workplace, trade or industry concerned except out and out scabs and fascists. This means trade unions inevitably and rightly contain large numbers of workers whose ideas are confused and on many issues downright reactionary.

Therefore there has to be a further level of workers' organisation, the political party, which wages the battle for revolutionary ideas, revolutionary strategy and revolutionary leadership within the trade unions as well as among other sections of society (the unemployed, students, full-time parents, etc) who are not in trade unions or in workplaces.

Those anarchists who do see the need for a coordinated struggle for revolutionary ideas and therefore form their own distinct anarchist organisations are in fact forming anarchist parties under another name. Their failure to recognise this openly is not an advantage which enables them to avoid the problems which beset other organisations but a disadvantage in that their confusion on this question, along with their confusion on the questions of the state and leadership, prevents them from pursuing any coherent strategy or having any clear idea of the role and structures of their own organisation.

The need for working class organisation and the uneven development of its consciousness are facts which can be denied only by those who think it is ultra-revolutionary to paint the working class in the most glowing and unrealistic colours. Therefore the most common anarchist reply is to argue that the record of would-be revolutionary parties shows that they inevitably degenerate into bureaucracy, elitism, authoritarianism and various other evils. "What guarantee is there", asks the anarchist, "that your proposed party won't go the same way?"

But of course there can be no absolute guarantee, just as there can be no absolute guarantee of the victory of the revolution, or the success of a demonstration or strike, or of anarchism for that matter. The only sensible way of dealing

ANARCHISM: A MARXIST CRITICISM

with this problem is first to establish the reason for the degeneration of so many workers' organisations and parties and then see what can be done to safeguard against it.

Anarchists commonly explain the degeneration of parties either in terms of the innate power hunger of leaders or the inherent authoritarianism of Leninist forms of organisation such as democratic centralism. The first explanation is self-defeating because if we are talking about "innate" tendencies then they will corrupt any association, group or society and make anarchism itself impossible. The second fails because it is clear that bureaucratic degeneration has affected not just Leninist parties but all types of workers' organisations including mass reformist parties and trade unions including the anarcho-syndicalist ones.

In contrast Marxists explain the tendency to degeneration by the pressure exerted on workers' organisations by the capitalist society within which they arise. This pressure is exerted at two levels. On the one hand the exploitation, oppression and alienated labour imposed on rank and file workers by capitalism make it difficult for them to develop the confidence and consciousness necessary to control their leaders. On the other hand capitalism by its nature continuously exercises a corrupting influence on leaders in such a way as to separate them, directly or indirectly, from the rank and file.

This explanation is especially important in accounting for what is undoubtedly the worst case of degeneration in the history of the revolutionary movement, the transformation of Bolshevism into Stalinism. On the one hand the pressure of world capitalism on the Russian Revolution in the form of an externally backed and imposed civil war effectively destroyed the working class that had made the 1917 Revolution. This class, which had in 1917 reached such heights of consciousness and confidence, was so smashed by war, famine, epidemic and total economic collapse that it was unable to continue to exercise its healthy democratic rule over society, and bureaucratisation of the leadership inevitably set in. On the other hand the pressure of capitalism on this bureaucratised leadership (symbolised by Stalin) seduced it into abandoning its orientation on international revolution (which alone could have saved the revolution) in favour of competing with capitalism on its terms, ie the establishment of state capitalist exploitation for the sake of competitive capital accumulation.[*]

The same pressures, though working in very different circumstances, also produce the domination of trade unions by their full-time officials and of reformist parties by their parliamentary representatives.

So how can a revolutionary party protect itself from these pressures which are always at work in capitalist society? Four measures are essential:

(1) The party must be involved in the day to day struggles of working people. It is this relationship which creates a counter-pressure to that exerted by capitalism. By contrast reformist parties base themselves mainly on the passivity of workers while sects do not establish a relationship with the working class at all.

(2) The party must adhere strictly to revolutionary principles.

---

[*] The question of the relationship between Leninism and Stalinism is obviously of great importance in the debate between Marxism and anarchism and I return to it in the discussion of anarchism in the Russian Revolution. For general Marxist accounts of Stalinism see Chris Harman, *How the Revolution was Lost* (1967) http://www.marxists.org/archive/harman/1967/xx/revlost.htm and Tony Cliff, *State Capitalism in Russia*, http://www.marxists.org/archive/cliff/works/1955/statecap/index.htm

This in itself will largely exclude both careerist elements and politically backward elements who are prone to manipulation.

(3) For obvious reasons no material privileges should attach to positions or leadership in the party.

(4) The party structure and rules must combine democracy (full discussion and debate on policy, election and accountability of leadership) with centralism (unity in action carrying out majority decisions). Centralism or discipline is commonly viewed, especially by anarchists, as a mechanism of authoritarian control from above. In fact in a revolutionary party it is just as much an instrument of democracy. It ensures the implementation of party policy by leaders, in contrast to non-democratic centralist organisations where leaders are "free" to disregard party policy or individualistically make it up.

In the final analysis it is the party's living relationship to the class struggle that is decisive and this cannot be guaranteed in advance by any constitutional structure. But this in no way alters the necessity of a party for revolutionary victory, and it is Leninist democratic centralism that offers the best means of resisting the constant pressures exerted on all working class parties by their capitalist environment.

Through its rejection of parties in general and the Leninist party in particular anarchism merely contributes to the organisational and political disarmament of the working class.

Individual, society and class

There is no doubt that one of the main differences between Marxism and anarchism has been over the relationship between the individual and society. In some ways this is trickier to deal with than the differences I have discussed so far. First it is of necessity more abstract and philosophical and second it is complicated by the deep division on this question that has always existed in the anarchist movement. Nevertheless individualist anarchism has been a sufficiently important tendency within the movement for me to have to deal with it and I hope that those anarchists who reject individualism for a class-based approach will appreciate that this section is not aimed at them.

Another reason for discussing this is that Marxism is commonly identified with a crude anti-individualism that condemns all concern for the individual as "bourgeois" and mechanically counterposes society and the collective to the individual. This is a misreading of Marx and the Marxist position, fuelled of course by Stalinism, and an impression I want to correct.

Individualist anarchism can be traced back to the English philosopher William Godwin (1756-1836) and the German philosopher Max Stirner (1806-1856), both of whom preached extreme individualism, a flavour of which can be gained from the following quotations from Stirner's book, *The Ego and His Own* (1845):

All Things Are Nothing To Me.

And will you not learn by these brilliant examples [god and mankind] that the egoist gets on best? I for my part take a lesson from them, and propose, instead of further unselfishly serving those great egoists, rather to be the egoist myself.

God and mankind have concerned themselves for nothing, for nothing but themselves. Let me then likewise concern myself for myself...

Away, then, with every concern that is not altogether my concern...

Nothing is more to me than myself!
(http://www.lsr-projekt.de/poly/enee.html#all)

I suspect that the direct influence of Godwin or Stirner on present day anarchism is close to zero but because a rather vague, not systematically formulated individualism is so often an element in anarchist thinking it is worth offering a few critical observations on extreme individualism, ie the idea of the "free" individual who pursues only their own aims without any constraint, regardless of others.

First it should be said that such pure, unconstrained egotism has never existed in human history. Humans are, and always have been, irreducibly social, that is dependent on each other. In hunter-gatherer society which, as we have seen, was stateless and had no separate political authority, individuals were by no means free to do as they pleased or just serve themselves. Hunting was a necessity imposed by nature and was a collective, cooperative activity. Individuals who refused to acknowledge their obligations to the group found themselves excluded from the group, which over an extended period was close to a death sentence.

The idea of "pure", do as you please freedom can only be contemplated so long as we ignore the sphere of production, but we cannot live without production of the necessities of life. It therefore tends simply to take production for granted, to "assume" that somewhere, somehow, the clothes on our backs, the food in our mouths, and so on, have been provided for us which, of course, is a highly elitist, bourgeois attitude. (In contrast Marx made the question of production the cornerstone of his whole theory of history.) The individualist anarchist has the option of arguing that we should *create* a society in which there is such an abundance of goods that there is more or less complete freedom to work or not work as we please, but this does not resolve the problem of agency, of who is going to create this society and how.

Second, it is clear from history that the social roots of this kind of individualism are deeply bourgeois. In feudal society the philosophical starting point was god, the church and the social order as ordained by god. It was with the rise of capitalism that individualism, as in Descartes' axiom, "I think, therefore I am", became the starting point. In the early modern political philosopher, Thomas Hobbes, the idea that human life was basically an individualistic "war of all against all" provided the justification for the anti-anarchist conclusion that what was needed was a strong state. Likewise bourgeois neo-classical economics makes the idea of "economic man", the individual rational egotist consumer, its point of departure. Moreover it is no accident that while anarchists may wish to give this individualist anti-authoritarianism a left wing slant, there is no shortage of conservative libertarians who make it a foundation for very right wing pro-capitalist neoliberalism.

In this context it also necessary to mention the late-19th century German philosopher Friedrich Nietzsche, who believed that the driving force in all history and human behaviour (and to an extent in the whole universe) was every individual's innate "will to power". Nietzsche was not an anarchist, and is more famous for his influence on the far right including the Nazis, but he may have read and been influenced by Stirner, and he has been a significant influence on late 20th century thinkers such as Michel Foucault, who, in turn, have influenced anarchism. It is clear that many anarchists accept some version of the will to power theory and certainly use it to explain the behaviour of others—Leninists, politicians, bureaucrats, etc—if not themselves. Also fitting well with this notion is the idea of the principle of the state or the principle of authority as the *creator* of class divisions and economic inequality, rather than the other way round as in Marx.

Apart from the fact that it lacks any empirical foundation, the idea of a universal will to power is basically a right wing theory. It can be given a left gloss and left appeal, as it is by Foucault, if it is used to analyse power and power struggles disbursed across society—in every school, hospital, prison and office—and accompanied by the voluntary choice to always resist power, to always side with the powerless. But there are two problems here. The first is that the best that can be hoped for is endless resistance, without any prospect of general liberation, since the power struggles will always renew themselves; the second is that if the will to power is innate and universal *why* should we, or anarchists, choose to side with the powerless, when it would be equally, perhaps more, reasonable to side with the powerful, as so many Nietzscheans have, in fact, done?

What then is the Marxist view of the relationship between the individual and society? Marxism does not at all reject concern for individual freedom and the development of the individual personality. In the *Communist Manifesto* Marx and Engels condemn capitalism for, despite its preaching of individualism, actually crushing the individuality of the majority:

> In bourgeois society capital is independent and has individuality, while the living person is dependent and has no individuality... That culture, the loss of which he [the bourgeois] laments, is, for the enormous majority, a mere training to act as a machine.

And they proclaim as their goal, "In place of the old bourgeois society, with its classes and class antagonisms...an association, in which *the free development of each* is the condition for the free development of all" (my emphasis).

Engels expands the point in *Anti-Dühring* (1877):

> It goes without saying that society cannot free itself unless every individual is freed. The old mode of production must therefore be revolutionised from top to bottom, and in particular the former division of labour must disappear. Its place

must be taken by an organisation of production in which, on the one hand, no individual can throw on the shoulders of others his share in productive labour, this natural condition of human existence; and in which, on the other hand, productive labour, instead of being a means of subjugating men, will become a means of their emancipation, by offering each individual the opportunity to develop all his faculties, physical and mental, in all directions and exercise them to the full (http://www.marxists.org/archive/marx/works/1877/anti-duhring/ch25.htm).

For Marx the individual is not an isolated egotist or "island unto himself" counterposed to society. In his *Economic and Philosophic Manuscripts of 1844* (Moscow 1981) he writes, "The individual *is the social being*" (p93) and criticises "*crude* communism" which is just concerned with the purely negative abolition of private property and "negates the *personality* of man in every sphere" (p88) in favour of communism "as the complete return of man to himself as a social (ie human) being...and the genuine resolution of the conflict...between the individual and the species" (p90) (Marx's emphases).

Reaching this "realm of freedom", however, requires an agent of change, a social force capable of overthrowing capitalism and building the new society. For Marx this agent of change is the working class or proletariat, "the class of modern wage labourers who, having no means of production of their own, are reduced to selling their labour power in order to live", as they are defined in the *Communist Manifesto*. This identification of the revolutionary role of the working class—its capacity to liberate itself and in the process liberate humanity—is the central idea in Marxism and it runs right through this booklet. I want to make two points about the relationship between working class struggle and individual freedom.

The first is simply that *any* collective struggle involves certain limitations on an individual's freedom to do as he or she pleases and that, as we have already noted, in the most elementary form of the working class struggle, the strike, the individual who pleases themselves by working is a scab. But the second is that there is a very significant difference between the middle class and the working class experience of individual freedom. For the middle class person their individual freedom and development are secured or advanced in opposition to the collective; for the working class person the main limitation on their individuality and freedom is their restricted economic situation and this can only be improved collectively. Consequently for the majority of working class people their individual development is dependent on the advance of their class as a whole. For example, their individual ability to live healthier and longer lives is dependent on the collective achievement of a free health service, their opportunity to get an education is dependent on the existence of free state education and so on. Indeed for many workers it is precisely in and through collective struggle that their individual personality awakens and flowers. A revolution involves the simultaneous awakening of millions of such individual personalities and the achievement of workers' power in society would mean—if not yet complete freedom—a huge expansion of individual freedom compared to anything that capitalism can offer.

Some tendencies in anarchism such as anarcho-syndicalism and communist anarchism have shared with Marxism this recognition of the role of the working class, but usually they have restricted themselves to abstract declarations in favour of freedom and not thought through the relation between working class struggle and individual freedom, as Marx and Engels did. Others have either rejected the notion of the working class altogether and thus cut themselves off from any social force that could actually bring about change or sought a substitute for it such as "the multitude" or "the precariat". These latter options will be discussed in the section on autonomism in chapter 4.

3. The record of anarchism

Elements of anarchist thinking can be traced back for centuries since human beings have always dreamt of a free and equal society, but anarchism as a defined ideology and movement dates, like Marxism, from the mid-19th century.

In the course of the 160 or so years of its existence there is no doubt that anarchism has produced its fair share, perhaps more, of heroes and heroines—individuals, both famous and unsung, who have given their lives to and for the revolutionary cause. There is also no doubt that the weaknesses we have identified have frequently shown themselves in anarchist practice.

It is obviously not possible to review here the whole history of anarchism. Instead I shall attempt to illustrate, and thus reinforce, the arguments already presented by reference to three episodes in the history of anarchism: Bakunin's activities in the 1870s; anarchism in the Russian Revolution (with a note on the anarchist critique of Bolshevism); and the role of anarchism in the Spanish Civil War. This is not a matter of scouring the anarchist record for examples of scandal, betrayal and idiocy—a pointless endeavour which can easily be duplicated for the history of Marxism—but of examining key moments in the history of the revolutionary struggle, which offer some of the high points of anarchist practice. It thus challenges the anarchist tradition on its strongest rather that its weakest ground.

Bakunin

Mikhail Bakunin (1814-1876) is perhaps the single most renowned figure in the history of anarchism. Certainly in his appearance, lifestyle and passion for action he appears as the archetypal romantic anarchist hero. Direct participant in a number of failed insurrections and veteran of many prisons including five years solitary confinement in the infamous Peter and Paul fortress in St Petersburg in Russia, Bakunin, more than any other individual, was the founder of anarchism as an organised tendency distinct from the broader socialist movement.

He also embodied with a peculiar intensity the contradictions inherent in anarchism as an ideology.

In his attacks on Marxism as "statist" and "authoritarian" and his many demagogic proclamations Bakunin presents himself as the radical opponent of all power, authority, leadership and subordination. Thus the programme of Bakunin's movement, "The International Brotherhood", states:

> With the cry of peace for the workers, liberty for all the oppressed and death to rulers, exploiters and guardians of all kinds, we seek to destroy all states and all churches along with all their institutions and laws, religious, political, juridical, financial, police, university, economic and social, so that the millions of deceived, enslaved, tormented and exploited human beings, liberated from all their directors and benefactors, official and officious, collective and individual may breathe at last with complete freedom (M Bakunin, *The Programme of the International Brotherhood*, 1869, http://www.marxists.org/reference/archive/bakunin/works/1869/program.htm).

In 1871 he declared, "In a word we reject all legislation, all authority, and all privileged, licensed, official and legal powers over us, even though arising from universal suffrage." And in 1872, "We do not accept, even for the purposes of a revolutionary transition, national conventions, constituent assemblies, provisional governments, or so-called revolutionary dictatorships."

Yet in his own political practice, Bakunin devoted himself to the organisation of small, secretive and hierarchical conspiracies founded on the principle of complete obedience to himself. Bakunin explained his methods in a letter to the notorious Russian conspirator Nechayev:

> Societies whose aims are near to ours must be forced to merge with our Society, or at least must be subordinated to it without their knowledge, while harmful people must be removed from them. Societies which are inimical or positively harmful must be dissolved, and finally the government must be destroyed. All this cannot be achieved only by propagating the truth; cunning, diplomacy, deceit are necessary ("Letter to S Nachayev", p34, http://quod.lib.umich.edu/l/labadie/29 16979.0001.001?rgn=main;view=fulltext).

It was these tactics which Bakunin employed in his attempt to win control of the International Working Men's Association or First International. When Bakunin and his supporters joined the International in 1869 they declared their own organisation, the Alliance of Socialist Democracy, dissolved but in fact maintained it as a secret network. In 1872 Bakunin wrote to an Italian supporter as follows:

> I think you will sooner or later come to understand the necessity of founding, inside [the sections of the International] nuclei composed of the surest, most devoted, most intelligent and most energetic members, in short the closest ones. Those nuclei closely linked among themselves and with similar nuclei which are organised or will organise in other regions of Italy or abroad will have a double mission. To begin they will form the inspiriting and vivifying soul of that immense body called the International Working Men's Association as elsewhere and next they will take up questions that it is

impossible to treat publicly... For men so intelligent as you and your friends I think I have said enough... Naturally this secret alliance would accept into its ranks only a very small number of individuals.

This contradiction between declared principle and actual practice should not be seen as simply a consequence of Bakunin's personal urges to dominate. In reality Bakunin is the living embodiment of the contradiction inherent in anarchism's rejection of leadership as such: namely that in place of democratically elected and removable leadership it puts undemocratic, unelected and irremovable leaders.

The secret conspiracy not only violated anarchism's own principles, but was also a disastrous method for leading working class revolution. No tiny band of specially selected individuals could possibly either gauge or guide the mood of the working class; therefore conspiracy led directly to putschism, the attempt by tiny minorities to stage insurrections independently of the actions or wishes of the majority of workers. Bakunin took part in several such ventures, all pathetic failures, including one at Lyons in September 1870 where, amid a wave of popular unrest, he and his supporters occupied the Hotel de Ville, declared themselves a Committee for the Salvation of France and announced the abolition of the state.

Unfortunately the state refused to recognise its abolition and promptly, in the shape of two companies of the National Guard, abolished Bakunin's coup. Bakunin was forced to flee, eventually to Genoa, and was thus excluded from participation in the real workers' revolution, the Paris Commune of the following year.

Interestingly Bakunin applied his concept of secret power not only to the organisation of the revolutionary movement but also to the organisation of post-revolutionary society. In a letter to his friend and follower Albert Richard, Bakunin explained how once anarchy had been established he and his supporters would constitute a "secret dictatorship":

> As invisible pilots amid the proletarian tempest, we must direct it, not by an open power but by the collective dictatorship of the Allies [Alliance members]: a dictatorship without any badges of office, without titles, without official rights and all the stronger in that it will have none of the appearances of power. That is the only dictatorship that I accept (cited in Hal Draper, *Karl Marx's Theory of Revolution, Vol III: The "Dictatorship of the Proletariat"*, New York, 1986, p95).

It is fortunate that this vision of invisible power can be dismissed as a complete fantasy since if it were to be realised it would be the most undemocratic form of rule imaginable.

Some latter-day anarchists may be tempted to disown Bakunin, but as we shall see, the fundamental defects of Bakuninism reappear in the anarchism of the 20th century even at its "greatest" moments.

Russia

The anarchist tradition predated the Marxist in Russia, but it is really striking how small the role of anarchism was in the revolution of 1917.

The Russian Revolution was the greatest and most profound revolution in history. The level of struggle and political consciousness achieved by the Russian workers and soldiers in 1917 was the highest achieved by any working class at any time, yet anarchism barely managed to get a foothold in this momentous movement.

Thus Voline, the most important Russian anarchist intellectual of the period, returning to Russia in July 1917, found not a single anarchist newspaper or poster or speaker in Petrograd (as St Petersburg had been renamed), the very heart of the revolution. In the soviets the anarchists had no representation worth speaking of and even in the grassroots factory committees anarchist resolutions were consistently lost to Bolshevik resolutions by overwhelming majorities.

There were two main reasons for this failure. The first was the role played by the Bolsheviks. In general anarchist moods develop among sections of the working class when the existing leadership of the workers' movement is at its most treacherous and disillusionment sets in, but in 1917 the Bolsheviks offered a clear revolutionary lead and thus attracted the support of virtually all working class militants.

The second was that from February to October 1917 there was a period of dual power, that is a period of struggle between two rival states. On one side stood the remains of the old tsarist state, with its army and bureaucracy, presided over by the new Provisional Government; on the other stood the soviets created by the workers and soldiers themselves and gaining in power and authority by the day. The crucial question—ultimately the only question—was which state representing which class would win. Would the old tsarist/capitalist state crush the soviets and the working class or would the working class smash the old state and transfer all power to the soviets? All political forces which vacillated on this question—the Kerensky government, the Mensheviks, etc—were steadily reduced to impotence. A tendency, such as anarchism, which rejected all states on principle, was necessarily marginalised. The majority of the anarchists who did exist either compromised their ideology and became lukewarm supporters of soviet power or broke with anarchism and joined the Bolsheviks. Those who did not, like the veteran Kropotkin (already discredited by his support for Russian, British and French imperialism in the First World War), became identified with the increasingly hated

Provisional Government.

In fact it was only some time after the October Revolution, in the civil war which followed, that anarchism was able to play a significant independent role in events. The civil war was a period of intense difficulties for the revolution and enormous suffering for the Russian people. The revolution was under siege. The White armies, led by the most reactionary tsarist generals, and backed with money, arms and troops by all the forces of international capitalism, came within a hair's breadth of capturing Petrograd and extinguishing the fledgling workers' state. Coming on top of the devastation of the First World War, the economic crisis of 1917, the inevitable disruption caused by the revolution itself, and the huge losses inflicted on Russia at the Treaty of Brest Litovsk, the civil war not only took a terrible toll of life directly, but also produced a complete collapse of the soviet economy. Industry ground to a halt, the transport system broke down, there was no fuel to heat the cities, workers were forced back to the countryside in search of food, and cholera and typhus epidemics raged wildly.

The fact that, despite everything, the Bolsheviks managed to hold on and emerge victorious is a testimony to the deep reservoir of support they had built in the Russian working class. However, in this situation anarchism was able to gain a hearing among sections of the working class, and even more so among the peasantry, disillusioned by the bitter privations inflicted on them.

Discontent was particularly rife among the peasantry. In 1917 the peasants had seized the land from their age-old oppressors, the landlords, and the Bolsheviks had endorsed this, thus linking the peasant revolt in the countryside to the proletarian revolution in the cities. But during the civil war the workers' state had been obliged to requisition grain from the peasants by force of arms. There was no choice about this—the only alternative was mass starvation in the cities and the utter defeat of the revolution—but it inevitably alienated the peasantry. While the war was at its height the immediate threat of the return of the landlords ensured the loyalty of the mass of peasants to the soviet state, but as the war drew to a close peasant anger boiled over. This gave rise to two phenomena of historical importance, associated with anarchism and claimed by the anarchist tradition—the Makhno movement and the Kronstadt rebellion.

Nestor Makhno was a young Ukrainian anarchist who gathered round him a peasant army which fought first the White Army and then the Red Army with great audacity and success until it was eventually suppressed by the Red Army at the end of the civil war.

Kronstadt was an island naval base which controlled all access by sea to Petrograd and whose sailors played a leading role in the 1917 Revolution. In March 1921 Kronstadt rose in armed rebellion against the Bolshevik regime, demanding an end to grain requisitioning and "soviets without communists". Fearing that the revolt could lead to a reopening of the recently ended civil war the Bolsheviks reacted ruthlessly, marching the Red Army across the frozen sea to take the island by storm in a bloody battle.

Both the Makhno movement and Kronstadt have been mythologised by anarchism as expressions of the true libertarian revolution of the people crushed by Bolshevik totalitarianism. The reality was very different.

Makhno may have had a fondness for grand anarchist proclamations but in practice he was an autocratic peasant leader and military commander given to the arbitrary execution of his opponents (especially communists) and wild drunken revels. Perhaps the most telling judgement on the real nature of Makhno and his movement is pronounced by the extremely sympathetic historian George Woodcock in his classic study *Anarchism: A History of Libertarian Ideas and Movements* (London 1975):

At heart he was both a countryman and a regionalist; he hated the cities and urban civilisation and he longed for "natural simplicity", for the return to an age when, as in the past of peasant legends, "the free toilers" would "set to work to the tune of free and joyous songs". This explains why, in a later phase, when the Makhnoists captured a number of fairly large towns they never really faced the problem of organising industry and never gained the loyalties of more than a few urban workers.

But there was another factor in the situation—the Revolutionary Insurrectionary Army. Theoretically, this was under the control of the Congress of Peasants, Workers and Insurgents, but in practice it was ruled by Makhno and his commanders, and like all armies was libertarian only in name. It used its own form of conscription and a rough and ready discipline was observed which left no doubt that Makhno was master and often involved swift and violent punishments... His debaucheries were on a Karamazovian scale: even his admirer Voline admitted them (pp396-397).

And the anarchist Voline complained:

Under the influence of alcohol, Makhno...lost control of himself. Then it was personal caprice, often supported by violence, that suddenly replaced his sense of revolutionary duty; it was the despotism, the absurd pranks, the dictatorial antics, of a warrior chief...which led to the formation of a kind of military clique or camarilla about Makhno (cited in Woodcock, p397).

Like Makhno the Kronstadt revolt adopted libertarian slogans, such as the call for a "third revolution", which attracted the support of anarchists, but it too was rooted in peasant opposition to the grain requisitioning of War Communism. The Kronstadt garrison of 1921 was not the garrison of 1917. Its class composition had undergone a major shift as the veterans of 1917 had been killed or moved and been replaced by new recruits from the countryside, many of them, like the 2,500 Ukrainians of the 160th Rifle Regiment, drawn from areas particularly friendly to Makhno. But the peasantry was not a social force which could lead the Russian Revolution forward. Allied to private property in the shape of the small farm, individualistic in its mode of production, geographically and economically isolated from the decisive forces of production in the cities, its material conditions of life made it impossible for the peasant movement to pose a national (let alone international) alternative to Bolshevik power.

Modern society cannot be ruled or organised from the countryside; the peasantry is forced to follow one or other of the main urban classes; either the bourgeoisie or the proletariat.

This general truth applied with particular force to the situation in Russia. Directed against tsarism and the landlords and allied to the workers' movement in the cities the peasant revolt was immensely progressive. Directed against workers' power in the cities or even the remnants of workers' power as represented by the Bolsheviks it was unavoidably reactionary. Regardless of whether the banner it raised was red, green or anarchist black, peasant revolt aimed at smashing "communist dictatorship" could only open the door to capitalist or tsarist restoration.

Strategically located at the entrance to Petrograd, the Kronstadt rebellion, had it triumphed or even survived for any length of time, would have given the recently defeated Whites a golden opportunity to reopen the civil war. The Whites understood this fully and bent every effort to get food aid to Kronstadt while making plans to send forces should the revolt succeed.

That Russian and foreign anarchists rallied to the support

of Kronstadt shows only that they were confused as to their own class allegiances, incapable of analysing the situation in class terms and blinded to reality by their utopian theory of a stateless, leaderless revolution.

Thus the balance sheet of anarchism in history's greatest revolution reveals that when the revolution was advancing it was irrelevant and when the revolution was retreating it gave unintended but nonetheless real help to the counter-revolution.

Note on the anarchist critique of Bolshevism

This booklet is a Marxist criticism of anarchism, not a general defence of Marxism. Nevertheless a significant element in anarchist ideology has always been its critique of Marxism as authoritarian and at the heart of that argument has stood its critique of Leninism and Bolshevism, in particular of the behaviour of Lenin and the Bolsheviks in the early years of the revolution. Since revolutionary socialists and Marxists who reject Stalinism (primarily Trotskyists) have generally defended the Bolshevik record in this period this has been an important question in the Marxism-anarchism debate. Considerations of space make it impossible to deal fully with these matters here (in my opinion the best account and analysis of the period is provided in Tony Cliff, *Lenin, Vol 3, Revolution Besieged*, London 1987) but a comment on the main issues is necessary.

The essence of the anarchist argument runs as follows:

(1) The revolution of October 1917 was a Bolshevik coup rather than a genuine workers' revolution.

(2) Rather than establishing the dictatorship *of* the proletariat (workers' power), the Bolsheviks established their own

dictatorship *over* the proletariat—they systematically concentrated power in their own hands, abolished workers' control in the factories, suppressed all opposition (as with Makhno and Kronstadt) and set up a one-party state.

(3) In this way Lenin (and Trotsky) laid the foundations for the monstrous Stalin regime that followed. Leninism led, and will lead again, to Stalinism.

The first thing to note about this view is how it corresponds almost exactly with the dominant bourgeois and right wing academic account of the revolution as offered by the likes of Robert Service and many others. This does not in itself refute it—after all I can agree with David Cameron that two plus two equals four—but on such a highly charged political question it should give anarchists pause for thought.

The idea that October 1917 was merely a coup gains credence from the fact that the seizure of power in Petrograd was carried out by only a few thousand Red Guards, and was completed in one night. But this ignores the huge support for the action among the mass of workers, including the fact that the Bolsheviks had by this time a majority in the soviets and the factory committees, and it spectacularly misses the point. The *reason* a few thousand Red Guards could capture the Winter Palace and arrest the government without immediately being repressed by the forces of the state was that the mass of soldiers, sailors and workers had *already* come over to the side of the revolution, leaving the Kerensky government with no one to defend it. Anyone who doubts this should try imagining what would happen if, tomorrow, a revolutionary party with a few thousand members (say the Socialist Workers Party) tried to march on parliament or Buckingham Palace and capture it.

The argument about the behaviour of the Bolsheviks in power is one sided but has some truth in it, in that they certainly did behave in a repressive manner—for example banning opposition parties. However, it leaves out the question of context and context makes a huge difference. If I say a famous revolutionary and self-proclaimed "friend of the people" shot a woman through the chest at point blank range, it sounds terrible. If we know that it was Marat in the French Revolution and the woman he shot was the counter-revolutionary Charlotte Corday, about to plunge a knife into his heart, it makes a difference. (Unfortunately Marat did not have a gun and was assassinated.)

Bolshevik authoritarianism was conditioned not by doctrine or innate inclination but by the circumstances in which they found themselves—circumstances of desperate civil war in which they were literally fighting for their lives and the life of the revolution. Moreover, it is crucial to understand that the civil war also utterly wrecked the Russian economy, producing a catastrophic fall in production, and it did so in such a way as to destroy the social base of the revolution, the revolutionary industrial working class. This left the Bolsheviks, as it were, suspended in mid-air and compelled to act in a dictatorial fashion.

The anarchist argument also takes no account of consequences. What were the concrete possibilities in Russian in 1920-21? One possibility, all too real, was victory for the White Guard counter-revolution, which without a shadow of a doubt would have meant the most terrible slaughter of workers, peasants and revolutionaries and some kind of Russian Nazism. Another concrete possibility was the Bolshevik dictatorship. Was a healthy, vibrant socialist democracy possible? No it was not, nor was a "normal" bourgeois democracy. The acute contradictions and desperate poverty and famine precluded both those options. Were an anarchist revolution and the rapid establishment of an anarchist society possible? Absolutely not! In these circumstances it is not surprising that revolutionaries, including such figures as the libertarian Victor Serge, opted for Bolshevik dictatorship, warts and all.

Of course it can be argued that the Bolshevik dictatorship led to "the most terrible slaughter of workers, peasants and revolutionaries" under Stalin after 1928, but the time lag is important. For the Russian Revolution the only way out of its impasse was to spread the revolution internationally. The strategy of Lenin and Trotsky was to hold onto power in the hope that international revolution could be achieved. In the event the international revolution was defeated, above all in Germany in 1923, and the consequence was full blown Stalinist counter-revolution. But that doesn't make the Lenin strategy wrong, especially as the main reason for the failure of the revolution in Italy, Germany and elsewhere was the absence of Bolshevik-type revolutionary parties.

To identify Leninism and Bolshevism in the period 1917-23 with the Stalinist state capitalist regime of the 1930s is to confuse a beleaguered distorted revolution with counter-revolution. A workers' revolution today, led by a Leninist party, would find itself in enormously more favourable circumstances in terms of economic development, the size of the working class and the chances of spreading internationally. It would be able to follow the path, envisaged by Lenin himself in 1917, of the party playing a leading role within a healthy multi-party soviet democracy and, indeed, the working class would have the power to ensure that it did.

Spain

If the Russian Revolution was the most momentous revolution of the 20th century, the Spanish Revolution of 1936-37 is among its closest rivals. Moreover, it is the only occasion in history when anarchism has entered a revolutionary upheaval already in possession of mass support. By 1936 the anarchist trade union federation, the

CNT, had a million members and was by far the largest tendency within the working class. The Spanish Revolution can therefore legitimately be regarded as a test case for anarchism—a test which it failed not through any defect in the anarchist workers who fought with supreme courage and self-sacrifice, but through inherent defects in anarchism as a revolutionary strategy.

The Spanish Revolution began in July 1936 in response to General Franco's fascist uprising against the newly elected Popular Front government (an alliance of the Communist Party, the Socialist Party and the republican bourgeoisie).

Despite the paralysis of the government the Spanish workers, predominantly anarchist in inspiration, rose magnificently to stop the fascists. Armed workers surrounded the army barracks in Madrid and Barcelona, calling on the soldiers to rise against their officers. After a day of fighting the barracks fell in Barcelona, then the next day in Madrid. Within days workers secured full control of the cities. Workers' committees sprang up to organise transport, food supplies, militias and healthcare. They sent armed columns to the countryside to secure food and support the movement of the agricultural workers. Collectively organising the running of society lifted everyone from decades of exploitation and oppression. In Barcelona, for example, the position of women advanced beyond that of any country in the world: abortion was legalised, birth control information made available, and a new free marriage without coercion or refusal of divorce instituted. As the writer George Orwell, who was there at the time, observed:

Above all there was a belief in the revolution and the future, a feeling of having suddenly emerged into an era of equality and freedom. Human beings were trying to behave as human beings and not as cogs in the capitalist machine (G Orwell, *Homage to Catalonia*, London 1984, p10).

The potential for successful workers' revolution was enormous but the fascist threat remained—Franco had succeeded in establishing control in the south west of Spain and another fascist, General Mola, was attacking from the north—so too did the Republican government, at least nominally still in power, in Catalonia (the heart of the revolution) and Madrid.

So what did the anarchist leaders do? (Note once again the existence in practice of anarchist leaders.) They joined the government—first in Catalonia in September 1936 and then in Madrid in December. This action was not only a departure from anarchist principles but also, more tragically, a betrayal of the working class and the revolution. The Popular Front government which the anarchist leaders entered was committed to the preservation of private property and the capitalist social order and to restoration of the authority of the Republican capitalist state. Its line was that there should be a broad cross-class unity of all democratic forces in the struggle against Franco and that the demands of the working class for fundamental social change should be shelved until after the fascists were defeated. For the bourgeois representatives in the government this position expressed the fact that for them the victory of fascism was ultimately a lesser evil than the victory of the working class and that therefore they would only collaborate with the left if their property rights were guaranteed. For the Socialist Party it expressed its long established willingness to collaborate with the bourgeoisie. For the Communist Party it was a policy imposed by Moscow so as not to alarm the French and British governments that Stalin was courting as allies against Hitler. Thus the anarchist leaders joined, and accepted responsibility for, a government whose conscious purpose was to clamp down on the mass uprising of the Spanish working class. It also meant accepting the responsibility for a strategy which, far from strengthening the struggle against Franco as it claimed, actually doomed that struggle to defeat.

If the war against the fascists was to be waged as a conventional military campaign then Franco, backed by the war machines of Mussolini and Hitler, was always going to win in the end. The only way for the anti-fascist forces to win was to transform the war into a revolution, give free rein to the energy and initiative of the masses, appeal to the workers and peasants in fascist-held territory through deeds as well as words and undermine Franco's base in Morocco (from which he launched his coup) by granting the colony its independence. The Popular Front government set its face against all this and was aided in the process by the leaders of anarchism, by far the largest tendency within the Spanish workers' movement.

The crucial question is why the anarchist leaders behaved in this fashion. Was it a purely individual aberration or was it a result of weaknesses inherent in anarchism? The answer is supplied by the CNT leaders themselves who, in seeking to justify themselves, referred to the exceptional nature of the situation (the threat of fascism) and explained:

> Either we collaborate or we impose our dictatorship... Nothing could be further from anarchism than to impose its will by force... We did not seize power not because we were unable but because we did not wish to, because we were against every kind of dictatorship.

In other words, the situation is desperate: the counter-revolution is at the gates; to resist it there must be leadership, coordination and power. That power can be either the existing bourgeois state or a workers' state, the dictatorship of the proletariat, but since we as anarchists reject the dictatorship of the proletariat we have no choice but to go along with the bourgeois state.

There is an iron logic at work here which is not confined to Spain in 1936 but which has applied, and will apply, in every serious revolutionary situation. Counter-revolution will always be at the gates; the real choice will always be bourgeois power or workers' power; to reject the dictatorship of the proletariat will always mean capitulation at the decisive moment. The example of Spain, the highest point ever reached by anarchism as a mass movement, is therefore neither an accident nor an aberration. Rather it strikes at the core of anarchism, showing its fatal inadequacy as a guide to revolutionary action.

4. Anarchism today

As in the past, anarchism today comes in a variety, one might say a bewildering variety, of forms (the same is true of "Marxism", of course). Rather than attempt an inevitably inadequate overview I intend to look at two trends, lifestyle anarchism and autonomism, which have been significant in recent years and which represent polar opposites within the movement. I will also add a note on "platform anarchism" and then move on to comment on some key tactical issues on which Marxists and anarchists tend to disagree, namely direct action, participation in elections and democratic decision making.

Lifestyle anarchism

By lifestyle anarchism I mean the amorphous ideology— there is no definite doctrine—which advocates or celebrates living or attempting to live within capitalism according to "anarchist principles". This usually involves opting out of paid employment and attempting to live more or less communally, often in squatted accommodation, where the "normal" rules and hierarchies of the system do not apply. Sometimes this is referred to as living "outside" the system, but since the system doesn't really have an "outside" any more, it is more accurate to speak of living in enclaves within the system or in its "cracks", to borrow the term used by John Holloway. Usually these enclaves exist in areas of low cost housing in the inner cities, such as Hackney in London or Kreuzberg in Berlin, but sometimes such small communities are established in rural areas. Along with lifestyle anarchism can go a range of cultural pursuits—

performance arts, including cabaret, clowning and other circus skills, contemporary visual art, music, etc—food fads, paganism and forms of "new age mysticism".

By its very nature lifestyle anarchism precludes any common line, policy, strategy or political philosophy but sometimes this community, or elements within it, do engage in collective action, demonstrations, campaigns and the like, including confrontations with the state.

A detailed critique of lifestyle anarchism, from the standpoint of social anarchism of the more socialist kind, has been made by the veteran American writer and activist Murray Bookchin. His book *Social Anarchism or Lifestyle Anarchism: An Unbridgeable Chasm* (AK Press 1995) polemicises in detail against various theories and "gurus", mainly of an irrationalist or anti-scientific persuasion, and condemns the whole phenomenon as petty bourgeois and "deliciously safe". But there is no need to repeat these arguments here because from a Marxist point of view there are two very simple and straightforward criticisms to be made of lifestyle anarchism.

The first is that it offers no strategy or perspective on how to change the world. Indeed it does not even seriously attempt to offer such a strategy. The question of how to defeat, as opposed to evade, the power of capital and the capitalist state is seldom even posed, let alone answered. The most that seems to be hoped for is that the anarchist lifestyle will prove so attractive that sooner or later everybody or a majority of everybody will follow suit. It is not clear that anyone really believes this, but nonetheless it needs to be said that this is a complete non-starter. There is a substantial proportion of the population—the ruling class and the upper middle class who are closely tied to them (senior managers, top state officials, etc)—for whom there is not the slightest possibility of adopting an anarchist lifestyle or ideology, and unfortunately these are precisely the people who control wealth and power in this society. Similarly, though for different reasons, there is no possibility of their adoption by the majority of working class people. Most working class people do not enjoy wage labour—it is alienated labour and they resent it even though they may not use the term; but for the overwhelming majority unemployment is an even worse scourge, plunging themselves and their families into miserable poverty and making them feel useless. This is proved by the fact that whenever the capitalist economy permits it the number of unemployed shrinks to a very low level.

Moreover, it should be said that workers' instincts are right in this both from the point of view of their political power and from an overall social point of view. The economic and political power of the working class derives not only from their numbers but crucially from their ability to organise at the point of production to hit bosses' profits and, ultimately, to form workers' councils and to take control of production altogether. Unemployment, therefore, weakens the power of workers as individuals and as a collective.

The anarchist lifestyle is also not generalisable because it is dependent in a thousand ways on productive paid labour—every anarchist squat or commune that uses a telephone, mobile, computer, car, bus, train, bicycle, gas, electricity, running water, metal cutlery and innumerable other artefacts, is linked into the productive processes of modern capitalism. The capitalist system is now highly globalised and can be taken over but not, by any significant number, opted out of.

This leads directly to the second main criticism of lifestyle anarchism which is that even as an option for a minority (perhaps as a pre-figuration of future society) the anarchist lifestyle is not permanently sustainable except for very, very few individuals. Anarchists, like socialists and everyone else in this society, are products of capitalism, have been socialised under capitalism, and are subject continually to the economic, social and ideological pressures of capitalism. As people get older, especially if they have children (who are also subject to societal pressure), these pressures intensify rather than weaken. Inevitably these pressures affect and undermine both the commitment of individuals within the anarchist community and the principles of the community as a whole. This will particularly be the case if members of the community become engaged in small self-employed or entrepreneurial activities. The general pattern, therefore, is for lifestyle anarchism to function as only a temporary episode in the lives of a minority living in the margins of capitalist society.

Autonomism

Autonomism is a political trend which has been influential in the global anti-capitalist movement. The movement is usually dated from the Seattle demonstration against the World Trade Organisation in November 1999 and reached its high points in the July 2001 Genoa demonstration and the European Social Forum in Florence in September 2002. Autonomism is sometimes seen as a Marxist current because its theoretical roots in terms of its main thinkers, Mario Tronti and Toni Negri, lay first in the Italian Communist Party (PCI) and then in the far leftist group of the late 1960s, Potere Operaio (Workers' Power). However, in terms of its actual theory and practice autonomism has been far closer to anarchism than to the "classical" Marxism of Marx and Engels (or Lenin, Trotsky and Luxemburg).

In the 1960s autonomism (then known as "workerism") focused on the struggles of militant industrial workers at the point of production, especially those in the car plants of northern Italy. These were contrasted sharply to the parliamentary reformism and compromises of the Italian CP and its associated trade union leaders, and counterposed to political, party and trade union struggle in general. Tronti and Negri developed a so-called "strategy of refusal" which celebrated not only unofficial strikes but also sabotage and absenteeism, which were seen as the working class "autonomously" refusing to collaborate with capital and thus undermining it.

Later, after the beating back of the Italian workers' movement in the 1970s and a general crisis of militancy on the Italian revolutionary left, Negri shifted his focus from industrial workers at the point of production to what he called the "socialised worker" with emphasis on the unemployed and other "marginalised" elements. Then, following his incarceration by the Italian state (on false charges of involvement with the Red Brigades) he produced, together with Michael Hardt, two books, *Empire* (2000) and *Multitude* (2004), which enjoyed for a while considerable success and influence in radical circles. Here I want to examine two ideas developed by Negri and shared by many who see themselves as autonomists or anarchists, which are not only erroneous but positively harmful to the left and the anti-capitalist movement in its broadest sense.

First, the idea that refusing wage labour is a revolutionary act. I have already criticised this in relation to lifestyle anarchism but Negri and the autonomists, precisely because they were militant activists, pushed it to an extreme which was utterly disastrous. They started not only to focus on the unemployed but to see waged workers as collaborators with the system. Negri wrote as follows:

Some groups of workers, some sections of the working class, remain tied to the dimension of the wage... In other words they are living off income as revenue. Inasmuch, they are stealing and expropriating proletarian surplus value—they are participating in the social labour racket—on the same terms as management. These positions—and the trade union practice that fosters them—are to be fought, with violence if necessary. It will not be the first time that a march of the unemployed has entered a large factory so that they can destroy the arrogance of salaried income (Red Notes, eds, *Working Class Autonomy and the Crisis*, London 1979, p110).

This notion, which was acted on by young militants, really did the bosses' work for them in splitting the working class, leading to physical clashes between would-be revolutionaries and trade unionists, and driving a wedge between the employed and unemployed.

Second, moving on from the idea of the socialised worker, Negri and Hardt proposed the concept of "the multitude" (in opposition to the idea of "the working class"). The multitude is a vague term referring to almost everyone not actually part of the ruling class, similar to the old term "the people". At first glance this seems unobjectionable as socialists and anarchists alike have always invoked "the people" in agitation. Moreover, many bourgeois sociologists (and some socialists) operate with far too *narrow* a definition of working class as only manual workers rather than those who live by the sale of their labour power, thus excluding white collar workers and making the working class appear to be a declining class in modern society.

Nevertheless the notion of "the multitude" is fatally flawed. What it loses sight of, indeed positively obscures, is the fact that among the innumerable victims of global capitalism there is a specific class with a unique ability to challenge and overthrow the system, namely the international working class. Identifying the working class in this way is a strategic not a moral judgement. It is not based on the belief that workers are "better" than other people or that they all have socialist consciousness or on a sentimental attachment to the past of the labour movement, but on their economic position as the principal source of the capitalists' profit, on their linkage to the key forces of production in society and on their concentration in large workplaces and cities.

The centrality of the working class was demonstrated yet again in the Egyptian Revolution in 2011. The Egyptian masses demonstrated, occupied the squares and streets and fought the police in their millions, and Mubarak continued to cling to power. But when on 10 to 11 February the demonstrations were complemented by a huge strike wave, the generals, previously loyal to Mubarak, decided they had to sacrifice the dictator to save the system.

Since its birth in the industrial revolution the working class has constituted the point of departure, social foundation and strategic anchor for the best of the left, socialist or anarchist, Trotskyist or syndicalist. In cutting itself adrift from this anchorage autonomism sets the stage for strategic aimlessness and numerous tactical errors.

The same applies to the notion of "the precariat" recently elaborated by Guy Standing. According to Standing the precariat is "the new dangerous class" which he contrasts to "the proletariat—the industrial working class on which 20th century social democracy was built":

> It consists of a multitude of insecure people, living bits-and-pieces lives, in and out of short-term jobs, without a narrative of occupational development, including millions of frustrated educated youth who do not like what they see before them, millions of women abused in oppressive labour, growing numbers of criminalised tagged for life, millions being categorised as "disabled" and migrants in their hundreds of millions around the world (http://www.policy-network.net/articles/4004/-The-Precariat-%E2%80%93-The-new-dangerous-class).

Standing claims (falsely) that the Egyptian Revolution and the recent upheavals in Spain and Greece were all led by the precariat, but he does not so much advocate the cause of the precariat as use them as a threat to demand his chosen reform of the provision by the state of a basic income for all. Standing himself is a leftish social democrat but this doesn't prevent his buzzword being adopted and used by many anarchists and autonomists.

The basic error this theory makes is that those who are termed the "precariat" are in reality part of the working class and a minority part at that (about 25 percent of the population), not a separate class counterposed to the proletariat and certainly not an alternative to it as the agent of social change or revolution. On the one hand Standing's definition of the proletariat as the industrial working class ignores the fact that there was always a significant proportion of the working class whose lives were characterised by extreme insecurity, especially during recessions and times of mass unemployment. On the other hand the working class is not just industrial or manual workers but also white collar workers. It is all those who live by the sale of their labour power, be they steel workers or teachers, construction workers or shop workers.

Consequently to try to make the so-called precariat the strategic base for a movement for social change is to divide the working class, to restrict the movement to a minority of the working class and of society, and to cut it off from the majority of the class who also contain that organised section of the working class with the most economic power, the greatest ability to hit capitalism where it hurts capitalism most by halting production. Marx called the proletarian movement "the self-conscious, independent movement of the immense majority, in the interest of the immense majority"—therein lay its ability to win. Basing the movement on a minority is, once again, a recipe for defeat.

In *Empire* Negri and Hardt also argued that the state had lost its importance as a locus of capitalist power. Globalisation had produced what they called a "smooth space" of pure capitalist power in which nation states and inter-state imperialist rivalry had ceased to be of significance. This pronouncement, coming as it did shortly before 9/11 and the ensuing invasions of Afghanistan and Iraq, was unfortunate in its timing, but it must be said that it was always false. At the simplest level Wal-Mart (and most other giant corporations) could not trade a day without the back-up of a state and its armed bodies of men—it would just get looted by the poor. At the level of the international economy over 90 percent of the top 200 global corporations continue to have a distinct national home base and close ties with particular national state machines. As the slogan put it, "There's no McDonald's without McDonnell Douglas."

The error of downgrading the importance of the state was compounded when it was taken a step further by John Holloway in his book *Change the World Without Taking Power* (2002). Where for Negri the state was losing its importance in the current epoch of "empire", for Holloway a focus on the state was the original and abiding mistake of the whole socialist movement since its inception. The whole idea of capturing state power, pursued alike by reformists and revolutionaries, social democrats and Bolsheviks, Communists and Trotskyists, was wrong because the state apparatus is inherently authoritarian and oppressive and "capturing" it would result merely in replicating the same oppression against which the revolution had been made. Instead Holloway argued for a strategy of establishing "autonomous" power bases independent of the state, as the Zapatistas did in Chiapas in Mexico in 1994.

As a criticism of the practice of Labour parties and other social democrats this has some force, but misses the crucial point insisted on by Marx after the Paris Commune and

Lenin in *The State and Revolution*—that the working class cannot simply "take over" the bourgeois state but needs to smash it. As an alternative strategy it has very little to recommend it. The Zapatista revolt was hugely inspiring at a moment in history when resistance was at a low point internationally and the world's rulers were engaged in self-congratulatory triumphalism over the fall of Communism, but it did not succeed in changing Mexico, never mind the world. Moreover, what was possible in the jungles of Chiapas is not replicable in Sao Paulo or Buenos Aires or Cairo or anywhere in the advanced capitalist world. Here there simply is nowhere that is beyond or outside the reach of the state, and no place that can be maintained indefinitely as an autonomous space if it is also a threat to capitalist power. We may try to ignore the state, but that does not mean the state will ignore us.

John Holloway presents his perspective of not needing to take power with a great deal of poetic revolutionary rhetoric about refusing to create capitalism through our labour and celebrating the "cracks" in the system, but in reality it is a reformist not a revolutionary strategy, and it provides radical cover for all sorts of NGOs, pressure groups and campaigns who very definitely want to avoid confrontation with the state, either because they are funded by it or because they have no intention whatsoever of overthrowing capitalism.

Platform anarchism

Platform anarchism is a small but interesting phenomenon. It derives its name and its ideas from the *Organisational Platform of the Libertarian Communists* (http://www.nestormakhno.info/english/platform/general.htm) written in 1926 by Nestor Makhno, Piotr Arshinov and other Russian anarchists of the *Dielo Trouda* (Workers' Cause) group in exile in Paris. It is of contemporary relevance because it inspires a number of small anarchist groups today including the Workers Solidarity Movement in Ireland and The North-Eastern Federation of Anarchist Communists in North America.

The Platform is a product of its authors' experience of the Russian Revolution and is strongly marked by this experience. Accordingly it attributes anarchism's weakness above all to its lack of any coherent principles of political organisation. It argues:

> Anarchism is not a beautiful utopia, nor an abstract philosophical idea, it is a social movement of the labouring masses. For this reason it must gather its forces in *one organisation, constantly agitating, as demanded by reality and the strategy of class struggle.*
>
> We have an immense need for an organisation which, having gathered the majority of the participants of the anarchist movement, establishes in anarchism *a general and tactical political line* which would serve as a guide to the whole movement.
>
> The only method leading to the solution of the problem of general organisation is, in our view, to rally active anarchist militants to a base of precise positions: theoretical, tactical and organisational, ie the more or less perfect base of *a homogeneous programme* [emphasis in original].

These are astonishing lines, for what is "one organisation" with "a general and tactical political line" and a "homogeneous programme" based on "precise positions" but a party, and a very Leninist sounding party at that?

Even more surprising is what the Platform has to say in its section on "The Defence of the Revolution":

> The social revolution, which threatens the privileges and the very existence of the non-working classes of society, will

inevitably provoke a desperate resistance on behalf of these classes, which will take the form of a fierce civil war…

As the Russian experience showed, such a civil war will not be a matter of a few months, but of several years.

However joyful the first steps of the labourers at the beginning of the revolution, the ruling classes will retain an enormous capacity to resist for a long time. For several years they will launch offensives against the revolution, trying to reconquer the power and privileges of which they were deprived.

A large army, military techniques and strategy, capital—will all be thrown against the victorious labourers…

In order to preserve the conquests of the revolution, the labourers should create organs for the defence of the revolution, so as to oppose the reactionary offensive with a fighting force corresponding to the magnitude of the task…

…As in all wars, the civil war cannot be waged by the labourers with success unless they apply the two fundamental principles of all military action: unity in the plan of operations and unity of common command. The most critical moment of the revolution will come when the bourgeoisie march against the revolution in organised force. This critical moment obliges the labourers to adopt these principles of military strategy.

Thus, in view of the necessities imposed by military strategy and also the strategy of the counter-revolution the armed forces of the revolution should inevitably be based on a *general revolutionary army with a common command and plan of operations* [my emphasis].

I have quoted at such length precisely because it is so surprising to read these lines from the pens of avowed anarchists. Not only have they conceded the essence of the argument for a party, but they have also, on the basis of the Russian experience, ie the experience of a real revolution, conceded the essence of the Marxist argument for a workers' state.

The authors (and their contemporary disciples) deny this, just as they deny that their "one organisation" with its "homogenous programme" is a party, saying they reject the "principles" of "the state" and "authority". But these denials are in vain. As Engels and Lenin insisted, the essence of the state is precisely "armed bodies of men". Like it or not, a revolutionary workers' army "with a common command" implies a state, just as it implies a certain amount of "authority". No amount of word play will get round this.

To anarchist comrades of a Platform persuasion a Marxist can reasonably say you have gained important insights—into the need for a single organisation based on a homogeneous programme, the need to deal with violent counter-revolution and civil war, and so on. These, however, cannot simply be fitted into an anarchist framework. Far better to build on them by giving them a serious theoretical foundation by means of Marx's historical materialism and by integrating them into the Marxist theory of the state, and of the party, both of which are more developed, more complex and, crucially, more democratic than maybe many anarchists realise.

Direct action

One of the issues on which Marxists and anarchists often disagree in the course of the movement is the use of "direct action". It is not easy to give an exact definition of "direct action" since the term is applied to a wide variety of tactics but in general it refers to protest or resistance actions that break or defy capitalist law such as street sit downs and blocking the highway, occupying buildings, breaking into military establishments, breaking windows and other attacks on property. Direct action can involve violence or be explicitly non-violent. Clearly forms of direct action can be and have been used by many different political and social forces ranging from the Civil Rights Movement in the US, to Greenham Common feminists, to anti-capitalist demonstrators in Genoa to students in Dublin and London. Workers going on strike and picketing or occupying their workplace are taking a kind of direct action. The far right and fascists can also engage in direct action, as when the English Defence League target mosques.

So in what way is this an issue that divides Marxists and anarchists? It is emphatically not the case that anarchists support direct action and Marxists oppose it—on the contrary there are many occasions when Marxists support and take direct action. Nevertheless there is a real difference. Anarchism has a tendency to make a fetish of direct action, to insist on it to the exclusion of other forms of action, and to disparage other forms of protest. With this goes a tendency to exalt the excitement, danger, courage, and attention-grabbing qualities of direct action *above* the need to involve and mobilise the masses. In contrast Marxists view the use of direct action as a tactic to be used when, but only when, it contributes to the main goal, which is the raising of the confidence, consciousness and struggle of the mass of the working class.

Obviously there can be no absolute rule here; it is a matter of judgement in concrete circumstances and we all make mistakes sometimes. Nevertheless I would argue that in general the Marxist emphasis on mass action is correct. Elevating the role of direct action by small minorities underestimates the ruthlessness and power of the system and its state apparatus. For example, the idea of the Italian Tute Bianchi (white overalls) that it would be possible to defeat or even hold at bay the police and the state by developing special tactics of street fighting (wearing padding, etc) proved a complete illusion when it was put to the test at Genoa in 2002. The state has at its disposal not only police with batons, horses, dogs, tear gas, etc, but also guns and an army with artillery and tanks. The only way the police can reliably be faced down in street confrontations is by massively outnumbering them as in Egypt, and the only way the capitalist state as a whole can be defeated is if it is confronted by workers in their millions, so that it breaks internally.

Mass demonstrations, even if they are completely peaceful, and even if they do not succeed in producing a change in government policy, still have an important role to play in the movement. For many working people they are their first introduction to politics, their first experience of collective action, and can have a powerful radicalising effect. They also enable people to get a sense of their collective power, overcoming the isolation and atomisation that the system tries to impose. So there need to be forms of action open to people whose consciousness is just developing and who are taking their first, perhaps hesitant, steps into the movement. Big demonstrations also have a significant propaganda effect, internationally as well as nationally. For example, the fact that *many millions* marched against the Iraq war in 2002-03, even though they did not prevent the war, sent an important message to the people of the Middle East that the mass of ordinary people in the West did not support the imperialist aggression of their governments. This helped the left in the Middle East argue against Islamist and terrorist currents and laid down a significant marker for future international solidarity.

Conversely, an obsession with direct action can lead to a separation between the dedicated minority and the less committed majority. The former can become cut off from the latter and develop the illusion that it is only the dramatic deeds of a tiny group of insiders that really count for anything. This substitutionism can be very damaging to a movement. Revolution is the self-emancipation of the working class in their millions and there are no short cuts to it.

For all these reasons the mobilisation of the mass of the working class must be the priority.

Participation in elections

Pretty much all anarchists reject participation in parliamentary and other official elections. They would regard this activity as bourgeois politics par excellence, as corrupt, fraudulent—inasmuch as capitalist society is dominated by capital and the rich regardless of who wins elections—and a recognition of the hated capitalist state. Marxism shares these criticisms of bourgeois democracy, denies the possibility of a parliamentary road to socialism, argues for a revolutionary overthrow of parliament and its replacement by workers councils, but nevertheless argues, depending on circumstances, for participation in elections.

This is because revolutionaries are engaged in a struggle for the consciousness of the working class, against the influence of the capitalist media and the capitalist political parties (including the reformist parties) and bourgeois elections are a terrain on which that battle has to be fought. They are by no means the most important terrain—the trade union struggle and strikes are much more important, for example—but they should not be ignored. We may not have illusions in the parliamentary system but millions of working people certainly do, including many who claim to be cynical about it. Consequently elections are a time when people's attention is focused on politics in a way that it is not in normal times, and therefore standing candidates in elections offers an important opportunity to put over socialist ideas to a large audience.

If revolutionary socialist candidates are elected to local councils or national parliaments the opportunities for effective propaganda are greatly increased—and not just propaganda in terms of leaflets, speeches (inside the chamber and out) but also propaganda in action by supporting strikes, going to picket lines, taking part in occupations and demonstrations and learning how to expose and subvert the sham democracy of the parliamentary talking shop from within. It is not, as we have said, possible to change parliament into a body which works for the working class and the people, but it is possible for a revolutionary to operate inside it as a tribune of the people.

Some people, both anarchists and other people who have been made cynical by the sickening lies, hypocrisy and venality of everyday bourgeois politics (and this is how it is in *every* capitalist country), will say that the moment an honest revolutionary sets foot inside the rotten parliamentary system they will inevitably become corrupted. There is, of course, a real danger of this, as there is with individuals who get elected to official positions in the trade unions, for the system puts people under heavy pressure to compromise and conform. The bourgeoisie has centuries of experience in corrupting working class representatives. Therefore the movement has to take precautions against being sold out, making sure that its candidates are aware of and armed against the pressures to which they will be subject and establishing mechanisms of accountability to the rank and file. Most importantly the movement or party has to ensure that its centre of gravity, the main focus of its political activity, remains extra-parliamentary, in the class struggle in the workplaces and on the streets.

Provided these precautions are taken, it is not beyond the realms of possibility for the revolutionary movement to find individuals with the political strength to serve the revolution and the working class inside the parliamentary citadels of the system. Indeed history has shown that this can be done. Karl Liebknecht, SPD member of the German Reichstag, opponent of the First World War, leader and martyr of the German Revolution in 1919, is the most famous example. Bernadette Devlin, elected member of the UK parliament in 1969-74 for Mid-Ulster who was jailed for her part in "The Battle of the Bogside" in Free Derry, and punched Tory minister Reginald Maudling in the House of Commons following Bloody Sunday, is another. There are many other lesser known figures.

The problem with the anarchist position of not standing in elections is that it abandons this whole field of politics to the bourgeoisie and to its faithful allies in the working class, the Labour and reformist parties. In this way it actually helps the reformists, who will betray the working class in any serious confrontation and who on a daily basis spread bourgeois ideas among the people, to retain their hold on working class consciousness. Worse still, in circumstances where working people are disillusioned by the experience of betrayal by social democratic and labour type governments, as happens repeatedly, there is the grave danger if there is no left alternative at the elections that people will turn to the right and to fascist parties. From Hitler down to the BNP the fascists have shown that they know how to combine parliamentary and extra-parliamentary politics. The left cannot simply wash its hands of elections and give them a clear run.

Decision making in the movement

In the organisation of any strike, campaign, demonstration or meeting decisions have to be made. This is inescapable. Some of the decisions are small-scale and largely practical—will the meeting be at 7pm or 8pm? Sometimes they are issues of principle—does this campaign support or oppose immigration controls? Sometimes what seem like small practical questions contain much larger political and strategic implications. For example a debate about the destination of a demonstration may really be an argument about whether the demo should be entirely peaceful or whether it should risk ending in confrontation with the police. In setting up any conference decisions will be taken about the agenda, the platform speakers and so on. So how are these decisions to be made?

One method, which happens all too often in radical movements, is to have one person who is "charismatic" or dominant and calls all the shots. This should be unacceptable to Marxists and anarchists alike. A method traditionally used in the working class and socialist movement is that of democratic voting. This allows for a certain amount of delegated authority to "leaders" or "officers" of one sort or another, but the basic principle is that the majority decides. In recent years many anarchists and autonomists have been drawn to decision making by consensus—only that on which everybody in the campaign (in the room at the time?) agrees is actually a decision. Which of these methods is best?

Undoubtedly decision making by consensus is ideal—when there is a consensus. Or it may be best when there is sufficient agreement for a consensus to be reached reasonably quickly. But it is a disaster when there is no consensus and no consensus is going to be reached. And these situations do and will occur. It is a disaster because either no decision gets made—and you can't (except in very exceptional circumstances) have a demonstration without a decision as to where and when it will assemble, or a conference without the venue being booked in advance—or the decision is made on the basis of one side wearing the other down by being prepared to argue indefinitely (which gives a huge advantage to those who don't have to get up and go to work in the morning). "Consensus" also allows a very small but inflexible minority to block and stymie a large majority and thereby paralyse a campaign or organisation.

Decision by voting also has its drawbacks. Votes can be rigged and unfairly influenced, and they can also be ignored. Nevertheless, democratic voting is an essential method in the working class movement. Let me give two examples to illustrate this. The first is a hypothetical but everyday situation in the life of the workers' movement.

Five hundred workers in workplace A have gone on strike demanding a pay increase of 10 percent. After a week the employers make an offer of 5 percent and the trade union officials recommend acceptance, saying this is the best deal available at the moment. The workforce is divided. Out of the 500 there are about 100 who definitely want to accept, and another 100 or so who equally definitely want to carry on the fight, believing there is more to be won. How can the matter be decided? There is no prospect of "consensus". If everyone just does what they want the strike will fragment and be defeated. The union official would like to order everybody back to work. No! There needs to be a vote. The employers and the state will favour a postal ballot so that the workers vote at home as individuals. We (militants, socialists, revolutionaries, etc) fight for a vote at a mass meeting following a debate, so that the arguments of the 100 militants have a chance of winning over the 300 undecided.

This is a tradition that has to be fought for and defended in the movement. Workers (and revolutionaries) have to get used to voting—and accepting it when they lose the vote. Of course there will be some votes that cannot and should not be accepted—there are exceptions to every rule—but in general the unity and development of any union, strike, occupation, campaign or party can only be preserved if people are prepared to accept being outvoted, without splitting or walking out.

The second example is an actual event of huge historical importance—the October Revolution of 1917. In the early hours of the morning of 25 October the Red Guards, under the direction of the Military Revolutionary Committee of the Petrograd Soviet (president, Leon Trotsky) started to seize key buildings in the city. The insurrection met virtually no resistance and at 10am the MRC issued a statement:

The Provisional Government has been overthrown. State power has passed into the hands of the organ of the Petrograd Soviet of Workers' and Soldiers' Deputies, the Military Revolutionary Committee, which stands at the head of the Petrograd proletariat and garrison.

At this point in time the old bourgeois Provisional Government was still holed up inside the Winter Palace. Meanwhile on the same day in the same city the All-Russian Congress of Soviets was assembling in the Smolny Institute, with delegates from workers' and soldiers' councils all over Russia. The insurrection had been conducted under the banner of "All Power to the Soviets". What attitude would the Congress take to the insurrection? How would the matter be decided? Consensus was out of the question—in the hall were outright opponents of the uprising who would shortly leave to join the counter-revolution, as well as people such as the Menshevik Martov who wanted a compromise. Obviously there would have to be a vote—in fact there was a series of votes. Trotsky, in his *History of the Russian Revolution*, gives some of the figures:

> The statistics of this Congress which assembled during the hours of insurrection are very incomplete. At the moment of opening there were 650 delegates with votes: 390 fell to the lot of the Bolsheviks...
> The Mensheviks, with the national group adhering to them, amounted to only 80 members—about half of them "lefts". Out of 159 Social Revolutionaries—according to other reports 190—about three fifths were lefts, and moreover the right continued to melt fast during the very sitting of the Congress. Towards the end the total number of delegates, according to several lists, reached 900...
> A straw vote taken among the delegates revealed that 505 soviets stood for the transfer of all power to the soviets; 86 for

a government of the "democracy"; 55 for a coalition; 21 for a coalition, but without the Kadets (L Trotsky, *The History of the Russian Revolution*, London 1977, pp1146-7).

If international capitalism is to be overthrown there will have to be many such congresses of workers' councils or similar bodies and many such votes. That is the second reason, along with the immediate demands of the class struggle, why the practice of democratic voting needs to be nourished in the movement.

All these divergences, between Marxism and anarchism, over lifestylism, autonomism, platformism, direct action, elections and voting, have a common origin. They derive from the fact that authentic Marxism has always been clear about its goal of international workers' revolution, and has tried to assess and think through all strategic and tactical questions from this point of view. Anarchism has always lacked that clarity and has consequently hopped around all over the place, sometimes pulled by the needs of the working class, sometimes by other social groups and sometimes driven by the emotions of its own adherents.

5. The way forward

The argument of this booklet can be summed up in a single phrase: "Anarchism cannot win". For all its lofty ideals, and all its heroism, anarchism lacks a serious strategy for overthrowing capitalism and realising those ideals. But we desperately need to win; the whole future of humanity is at stake.

Not only is the current state of the world unacceptable—with 358 billionaires controlling as much wealth as the bottom half of the world's population; with a billion people going hungry while over $1,500 billion is spent on arms; with the bill for the bankers' economic crisis being presented to the working people and poor of the US, Greece, Portugal, Spain, France, Britain, Ireland, Iceland and the rest; with war, torture, racism, oppression and repression on every side—but if capitalism is left in place it will get worse.

The crisis of capitalism that broke in 2008 shows no sign of abating. On the contrary, after small signs of recovery—much played up by the media—it is evidently deepening again. The Eurozone staggers from calamity to calamity and bail-out to bail-out as Ireland, Greece, and now Italy and Spain teeter on the edge of default and meltdown. Obama and the US politicians are playing chicken as the US debt heads towards the symbolic limit of $14 trillion. China, the great economic success story of modern times and hoped for saviour of the world economy, is starting to slow down and worrying about inflation. Meanwhile at the other end of the system ten million people are facing famine in the Horn of Africa.

Leaving aside the ongoing consequences of the economic crisis, which include the growth of fascism in many countries and the possibility of ever more destructive imperialist wars, there is the ticking bomb of environmental catastrophe. If climate change is allowed to continue—and there is very little likelihood that capitalism, driven by competition and greed for profit, will stop it—the horrifying consequences for humanity could dwarf anything we have seen in history. Flooding like that in New Orleans, Pakistan and Bangladesh on a much vaster scale; drought and hunger like that in Darfur, the Sahel, Ethiopia and the Horn of Africa on a much vaster scale; wars for resources (water instead of oil) on a much vaster scale; refugees from all of these disasters on a much vaster scale. And if we want to know how capitalism will react to these events, just look at how the world's richest capitalist country reacted to Hurricane Katrina in New Orleans.

So the question of a strategy that really has a chance of winning—no one can offer guarantees—is of the utmost importance. The first thing such a strategy has to do is identify a real social force that has the capacity to change the world. Without that the best tactics, the noblest goals, the most daring plans are so much hot air and wishful thinking. The fact that Marxism identifies such a force—the international working class—is its greatest strength and Marx's greatest theoretical achievement.

By the working class Marx meant those who live by the sale of their labour power, employed and exploited by the capitalists. What made Marx base his politics on the working class was not its suffering but its power. The suffering and exploitation of the working class are, of course, appalling and they give workers the motive and the interest in challenging the system, but slaves and peasants have suffered and been exploited for millennia. What distinguishes the working class is (a) its power actually to defeat capitalism, and (b) its ability to create a new society.

The working class is the unique child of capitalism. As capitalism expands so does the working class. Capitalism can defeat the working class in battle after battle, break its strikes, smash its unions, curtail its liberty, but it cannot do without it to produce its profits, so always the workers return to fight again.

Capitalism draws workers together in large workplaces, links them in national and global industries, and concentrates them in vast cities. This gives them massive potential political power. Without their work no train, bus or lorry moves; no coal, iron or oil leaves the earth; no papers are printed; no TV station broadcasts; no bank or school opens. Even the armed forces of the state depend on workers in their ranks. In creating the working class, capitalism creates the most powerful oppressed class in history.

The struggle of the working class is, by its nature, a collective struggle. From the smallest local campaign to the largest strike against a giant corporation or a general strike against the government, workers have to act together. Indeed this collectivism can be a source of frustration for the individual militant or revolutionary, as workers in a workplace can only act when a majority of them are prepared to move together, but it is what makes the working class a socialist class. To take possession of the means of production the workers cannot divide them up between them (as peasants divided the land) but have to turn them into social property

Moreover, when the working class takes power it remains the producing class in society, with no class below it which it can exploit or live off. And being concentrated in big industry and big cities at the centre of economic and political power, it has the capacity to prevent any new class emerging above it; it will be able to produce and rule at the same time, thus laying the foundation for a genuinely classless society. In liberating itself the working class liberates humanity.

The revolutionary role of the working class is the core of Marxism. No proposition in Marx has been so roundly dismissed by academics and pundits, including those otherwise "sympathetic" to Marxism. "The working class has changed", is their familiar cry.

Yes, the working class has changed in its jobs, its clothes, its pay, its nationalities and its culture. But in its fundamental conditions of existence it remains: it is still the child of capitalism, still living by the sale of its labour power, still exploited and still struggling collectively—while in its size and potential power it has grown enormously. In Marx's day the proletariat was more or less confined to western Europe. Today it stretches to, and fights on, all five continents, from São Paulo to Seoul, from Canton to Cairo. Therein lies the hope for humanity.

But experience has shown, and it is now a long and bitter experience, that the working class can fight but to win it needs organisation and leadership and that means above all a revolutionary party. In other words it needs precisely those things anarchism, in all its forms, would deny it. The working class has risen against capitalism on so many occasions in so many places (Paris in 1848, 1871, 1936 and 1968; Germany in 1919-23; Italy in 1919-20; China in 1925-27; Spain in 1936; Hungary in 1956 against Stalinist state capitalism; Bolivia in 1952; Chile in 1970-73; Portugal in 1974 and so on) and time and again it has been deflected or defeated, often in blood. So far we have one real, albeit temporary, victory—the Russian Revolution of 1917 until it was usurped by Stalinism—and the factor that made the difference was the existence of a revolutionary party with serious roots in the working class.

Such a party cannot be built in a day. Again experience has shown that it is nigh on impossible to improvise it in heat of the revolutionary crisis. Rather it must be painstakingly constructed in advance of the revolution. It has to draw together, independently of the reformists and the trade union bureaucrats, the best fighters in the working class in every workplace and every housing estate. It has to equip itself with the ability to unite the rest of the class in struggle; it has to know how to advance and how to retreat and how to work with people outside its own ranks, including sometimes the reformists (and, of course, the anarchists), and when to strike the decisive blow. It has to have learned the lessons of history and be able to apply them to today.

And this is where Marxism comes in again for, as well as being a critique of capitalism and a vision of the socialist future, Marxism is a generalisation from the historical experience of the class struggle. The way forward, therefore, for those who want to change the world is to build the workers' movement, develop the workers' resistance and in the process construct a revolutionary socialist party based on Marxism.

Suggestions for further reading

Books marked OP are out of print, but should be available secondhand or in electronic form.

On Marxism as a whole

Chris Harman, *How Marxism Works* (Bookmarks 1997)
Alex Callinicos, *The Revolutionary Ideas of Karl Marx* (Bookmarks 2010)
Kieran Allen, *Marx and the Alternative to Capitalism* (Pluto 2011)
John Molyneux, *What is the Real Marxist Tradition?* (available online)

On the state

VI Lenin, *The State and Revolution* (various editions available)
Frederick Engels, *The Origin of the Family, Private Property and the State* (various editions available)
Karl Marx, *The Civil War in France* (various editions available)

On leadership and the party

Tony Cliff, Chris Harman, Duncan Hallas, Leon Trotsky, *Party and Class* (Bookmarks 1996)
John Molyneux, *Marxism and the Party* (Bookmarks 1986; Haymarket 2003)